BAKING
MASTERCLASS

YOUR ESSENTIAL STEP-BY-STEP
TO EVERY CAKE AND BAKE YOU NEED

HarperCollins*Publishers*

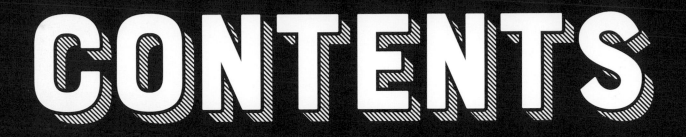

CONTENTS

HELLO!

When it comes to cakes and desserts, it's safe to say the food team at taste.com.au have dreamed up, developed, written and tested some truly amazing recipes. Led by baking queen and Taste's very own food director Michelle Southan, there's nothing they can't do, and we're thrilled to share so many favourites in this beautiful book.

Ranging from simple scones to towering layered creations, these recipes all have one key thing in common: each and every one is tried, tested, trusted and rated by the millions of people who use and review taste.com.au every month. Plus, as always, we've used supermarket ingredients to make shopping easy and affordable.

The recipes in this book have all the info you need to help you make the most perfect bakes, whether you're a novice baker or seasoned pro. We've included step-by-step pictures and tips so every question is covered, from how to line your tin with pastry to what consistency your meringue should be. The only tip we'd add? If you're making a recipe for the first time, read it all the way through and assemble your ingredients before starting, so you don't realise you're missing something after you've begun!

Baking Masterclass has every occasion covered, from gooey puddings to follow a family dinner to treats for the bake sale and special occasion cakes that are guaranteed to wow the crowd. Have a wonderful time baking and sharing.

**BRODEE MYERS,
EDITOR-IN-CHIEF**

HOW TO USE
BAKING
MASTERCLASS

Welcome to taste.com.au's *Baking Masterclass*, with all the recipes, tips and know-how you need to create beautiful cakes, biscuits, puddings and more.

AMAZING FEATURES

Full prep & cooking times

5-star recipe ratings

At-a-glance prep times

Reviews from home cooks

KEY GUIDES
Highlighted dots indicating freezable, kid friendly, make ahead, gluten free and easy

COOK'S TIPS
Helpful hints and insider knowledge courtesy of our expert food team

Extra info and tips to get the best results

Fun flavour twists

INFO AT A GLANCE

Use the icons to find the best choices for you and your family (such as freezable, kid friendly, make ahead, easy and gluten free – or all five at once). Just follow the highlighted dots, or turn to our index, which starts on page 248.

● GLUTEN FREE ● MAKE AHEAD ● FREEZABLE ● KID FRIENDLY ● EASY

EASY TREATS

Looking for a quick and easy bake for the cake stall or a fun treat to make with the kids? Here you'll find all your favourite biscuits, slices, brownies, cheat's desserts and sweet bites that will keep the crowds happy!

THE TASTE.COM.AU GUARANTEE

All taste.com.au recipes are triple-tested, rated and reviewed by Aussie cooks just like you. Plus, every ingredient is as close as your local supermarket.

AT-A-GLANCE
SWEET INSPIRATION

From classic pastries to celebration cakes, here's a little taster of what's inside.

Classic chocolate éclairs **p52**

Apple & custard tea cake **p22**

Malteser cheesecake slice **p178**

Fairy bread cheesecake Swiss roll **p134**

Profiteroles with chocolate **p98**

Flake cake with swirls **p138**

Lemon custard tea cakes **p234**

Jumbo iced VoVo tart **p184**

Choc mousse sticky date trifle **p226**

Molten chocolate soufflé **p106**

Passiona curd pavlova **p118**

Madeleines with choc drizzle **p245**

Brownie cheesecake stack **p126**

Buttery cookies with funfetti **p242**

Jam & vanilla cream lamingtons **p56**

Frying pan choc-chip cookie **p240**

Choc caramel popcorn cake **p142**

Raspberry & custard tart **p42**

Baci stack with fault line **p158**

Gingerbread cheesecake log **p222**

Chocolate lava puddings **p38**

Choc-cherry profiterole wreath **p198**

Chocolate zebra cake **p174**

Lemon curd cheesecake pav **p170**

Cherry ripe cupcakes **p162**

White Christmas lamingtons **p194**

Vanilla slice & honeycomb crunch **p146**

Gooey funfetti blondies **p232**

Dark chocolate mousse cake **p18**

Cheesecake chocolate bundt **p166**

Salted caramel pretzel cake **p114**

BEST OF THE CLASSICS

WHETHER YOU WANT THE ULTIMATE MUD CAKE,
A DREAMY LEMON MERINGUE PIE, PERFECT PROFITEROLES
OR A LUSCIOUS CREME BRULEE, THIS CHAPTER
HAS IT ALL, AND MORE!

STICKY NUT BANANA
MUFFINS

Make these super-easy banana muffins for lunch boxes or picnics, or up the stakes with a simple yet impressive topping!

MAKES 12 **PREP** 20 mins (+ cooling) **COOK** 45 mins

265g (1¾ cups) plain flour
155g (¾ cup) caster sugar
1 tsp baking powder
¼ tsp bicarbonate of soda
¼ tsp sea salt
½ tsp ground cinnamon, plus extra, to dust
1 vanilla bean
3 ripe large bananas, mashed well, plus sliced banana, to serve
2 eggs, lightly whisked
125g unsalted butter, melted
2 tbs milk
Double cream, to serve
STICKY PINE NUT TOPPING
70g pine nuts
70g dried coconut flakes
100g golden syrup
Pinch of sea salt

1 Preheat the oven to 180°C/160°C fan forced. Place an oven rack in the middle of the oven. Line twelve 125ml (½-cup) muffin pans with paper cases.

2 Combine flour, sugar, baking powder, bicarb, salt and cinnamon in a large bowl. Use a small sharp knife to split the vanilla bean in half and scrape the seeds into the flour mixture. Discard bean.

3 Combine the mashed banana, egg, butter and milk in a jug. Pour into the flour mixture, using a large metal spoon to gently fold together until just combined. Do not over-mix.

4 Spoon batter among the prepared pans. Bake for 20-25 minutes or until a skewer inserted into the centre of a muffin comes out clean. Transfer muffins to a wire rack to cool completely.

5 Meanwhile, for the sticky pine nut topping, line a baking tray with baking paper. Combine the pine nuts, coconut, golden syrup and salt in a bowl. Spread onto the prepared tray. Bake for 15-20 minutes or until golden and crisp. Set aside to cool completely.

6 To serve, spoon a small dollop of double cream onto each muffin. Top cream with the sliced banana, sprinkle with sticky pine nut topping and dust with extra cinnamon.

COOK'S TIPS

You will need about 1½ cups of mashed banana for this recipe.

○ GLUTEN FREE ○ MAKE AHEAD ○ FREEZABLE ● **KID FRIENDLY** ● **EASY**

★ ★ ★ ★ ★

*Perfect. So easy, I didn't
even need a mixer.*

NATALIEMULLAN

STEP-BY-STEP HOW-TO GUIDE

These tips will help you achieve fluffy muffins and a perfect crunchy nut topping.

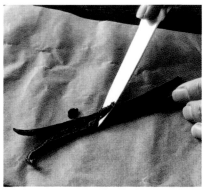

1 To remove seeds from a vanilla bean, use a small sharp knife to split the bean lengthways and scrape the seeds.

2 Try not to over-mix the batter when combining wet and dry ingredients or the texture will be dense and not fluffy.

3 Once baked, the pine nut topping will set as it cools. Let it cool completely before breaking it up.

DARK CHOCOLATE MOUSSE CAKE

This dense chocolate brownie fudge cake topped with light and fluffy mousse always hits the sweet spot. Make it ahead to serve at your next dinner party.

SERVES 12 **PREP** 45 mins (+ 7 hours chilling) **COOK** 40 mins

50g unsalted butter, chopped, plus extra melted butter, to grease
60g dark cooking chocolate, finely chopped
100g (½ cup) caster sugar
60ml (¼ cup) hot water
50g (⅓ cup) plain flour
40g (¼ cup) self-raising flour
1 tbs cocoa powder
1 egg

CHOCOLATE MOUSSE
500g dark cooking chocolate, finely chopped
750ml (3 cups) thickened cream

CHOCOLATE GLAZE
200g dark chocolate, finely chopped
185ml (¾ cup) thickened cream
2 tbs liquid glucose

1 Preheat oven to 160°C/140°C fan forced. Release base of a 22cm (base measurement) springform pan. Invert. Line base with baking paper. Secure in pan, allowing edge to overhang. Grease side with melted butter

2 Melt chopped butter, chocolate, sugar and water in a heatproof bowl over a saucepan of simmering water (don't let the water touch the bowl). Remove from the heat. Stir in flours, cocoa and egg. Pour into prepared pan. Bake for 25 minutes or until a skewer comes out clean. Cool cake completely in pan.

3 For the mousse, place chocolate in a heatproof bowl over a saucepan of simmering water (don't let the water touch the bowl). Stir for 3-4 minutes or until melted and smooth. Remove from the heat and set aside to cool slightly. Use electric beaters to beat the cream in a bowl until soft peaks form. Fold one-third of the cream into the chocolate mixture. Repeat twice until well combined.

4 Spoon mousse into the pan on top of the cake. Tap on the bench a few times to remove any air pockets. Use a spatula to smooth the surface. Place in the fridge for 6 hours or overnight to chill and set.

5 For the glaze, combine the chocolate, cream and glucose in a small saucepan over low heat. Stir until melted and smooth. Cool slightly. Pour over mousse. Place in the fridge for 1 hour to set. Serve.

COOK'S TIP

For a photo-finish slice, allow it to reach room temperature to bring back the shine, and cut the cake with a hot knife. Clean the knife between each slice.

○ GLUTEN FREE ● **MAKE AHEAD** ○ FREEZABLE ○ KID FRIENDLY ○ EASY

45 minutes prep

★★★★★ Made this cake for family and friends. We talked about it long after it was finished. Will be making it again, its a top favourite. An absolute gold medal winner. **WEENIE59**

STEP-BY-STEP
HOW-TO GUIDE

This impressive make-ahead cake is perfect for easy entertaining.

1 It helps to invert the base of the springform pan, so the lip doesn't get in the way when removing the cake later on. When lining with baking paper, don't trim the paper – it will help you remove the finished cake from the pan.

2 The cake layer is quite shallow, so don't worry if it looks like there's not enough mixture in the pan. To see if it's cooked, insert a cake tester or thin skewer into the centre of the cake. It should come out clean.

3 When melting chocolate, the water should be just simmering, not boiling. The bowl and spoon need to be completely dry before you start, otherwise the chocolate may seize and become grainy.

4 Gently folding the whipped cream into the chocolate is what creates the light texture of the mousse. It's important to let the melted chocolate cool slightly, then fold in the cream in batches to keep it as airy as possible.

5 After spooning in the mousse, tapping the tin on the bench will remove any air pockets in the mixture. If you don't have an offset spatula or palette knife to smooth the surface, use the back straight edge of a butter knife.

6 When you pour it over the cake, the glaze should have the consistency of caramel, and it will then set in the fridge, like a ganache. To serve the cake, release the side of the pan, then remove using the baking paper.

★★★★★ *I have made this recipe heaps of times and it's always really good.* **JELLYSPY**

APPLE & CUSTARD TEA CAKE

The simple things in life are best – like this butter cake with a scrumptious layer of custard and apples. Did someone say it's time for afternoon tea?

SERVES 8 **PREP** 20 mins (+ cooling) **COOK** 1 hour 10 mins

125g butter, at room temperature
100g (½ cup) caster sugar
1 tsp vanilla extract
2 eggs
300g (2 cups) self-raising flour
75g (½ cup) plain flour
85ml (¾ cup) milk
290g (1 cup) drained canned apple slices pie fruit
50g (½ cup) flaked almonds
1 tbs raw sugar
Double cream, to serve
CUSTARD
50g (⅓ cup) custard powder
435ml (1¾ cups) milk
2 tbs caster sugar
1 tsp vanilla extract

1 To make the custard, stir the custard powder and 125ml (½ cup) milk in a saucepan until smooth. Place over medium heat, stir in the sugar, vanilla and remaining milk, and cook, stirring constantly, for 5 minutes or until thick. Cool slightly.

2 Preheat oven to 180°C/160°C fan forced. Grease a 22cm springform pan. Line base and sides with baking paper.

3 Beat the butter, caster sugar and vanilla in a bowl until pale. Add eggs, 1 at a time, beating well after each addition. Fold in flours and milk until combined. Spoon half the cake mixture into the prepared pan. Smooth the surface.

4 Dollop warm custard over the cake mixture. Use the back of a spoon to spread evenly. Top with apple slices.

5 Dollop the remaining cake mixture over the top. Use the back of a spoon to gently smooth the surface to cover.

6 Sprinkle with almonds and raw sugar. Bake for 1 hour or until a skewer inserted into the centre comes out clean. Cool in pan for 20 minutes, then transfer to a wire rack to cool completely. Serve with cream.

COOK'S TIP

You could use canned peach or pear slices instead of the apple, if you prefer.

★★★★★ *I made this cake today for Father's Day and it was a hit! Everyone loved it and are already requesting it again. Must-try recipe!* **NESSA13**

○ GLUTEN FREE ● MAKE AHEAD ○ FREEZABLE ● KID FRIENDLY ● EASY

STEP-BY-STEP
HOW-TO GUIDE

These simple tips will make sure your cake turns out perfectly.

1 When preparing the vanilla custard, you'll know it's thick enough when it coats the back of a wooden spoon. The custard will thicken further into a spreadable consistency as it cools slightly, while you preheat the oven.

2 Use electric beaters or the whisk attachment on a stand mixer to beat the butter mixture and beat until the mixture has turned pale yellow and you can't feel the grains of sugar – about 2 to 3 minutes.

3 Use a wooden spoon to gently fold in the flour and milk, being careful not to over-mix, otherwise the batter may become tough. Then spoon half the mixture into the pan, in a smooth even layer.

4 After spreading the custard over the bottom cake layer, arrange the apple slices over the top in a single layer, using any smaller pieces to fill any large gaps.

5 Gently dollop the remaining cake mixture over the apple layer and gently smooth the surface with a spoon or palette knife to cover (don't worry if there's a few small gaps).

6 The almonds and raw sugar will create a golden crust for your cake, with a little crunch. If the top looks like it's getting too dark during baking, cover the top loosely with foil.

★★★★★ *If you like apple pie or crumble with custard, you'll love this. I made it for morning tea at work and everyone raved about it.* **HARMONYPUFFIN**

LEMON MERINGUE PIE

This lemon meringue pie is a lip-smacking delight! Smooth and silky, the lemon filling has sweetness and tang to tingle the tastebuds.

SERVES 10 **PREP** 20 mins (+ standing, resting & chilling) **COOK** 1 hour 30 mins

7 eggs, lightly whisked
310ml (1¼ cups) thickened cream
215g (1 cup) caster sugar
185ml (¾ cup) fresh lemon juice
1½ tbs finely grated lemon rind
225g (1½ cups) plain flour
125g butter, chilled, chopped
2 tbs icing sugar mixture
1 egg yolk
1-2 tbs chilled water

MERINGUE

315g (1½ cups) caster sugar
4 egg whites, at room
   temperature
Pinch of cream of tartar

1 Place the eggs, cream, sugar, lemon juice and rind in a large bowl and whisk until well combined. Cover and place in the fridge for 1 hour to develop the flavours.

2 Meanwhile, place the flour, butter and icing sugar in a food processor and process until the mixture resembles fine crumbs. Add egg yolk and water, a little at a time. Pulse to bring pastry together. Wrap in plastic wrap. Place in the fridge for 30 minutes.

3 Preheat oven to 200°C/180°C fan forced. Roll out the pastry on a lightly floured surface to a 4mm-thick disc. Use pastry to line a 5cm-deep, 25cm (base measurement) straight-sided pie dish. Trim the excess. Press the pastry slightly around the edge so it extends about 2mm above the edge of the dish.

4 Line the pastry shell with baking paper and fill with pastry weights or uncooked rice or beans. Blind-bake the pastry for 15 minutes or until the pastry is lightly golden. Remove paper and weights. Bake for a further 5 minutes. Set aside to cool.

5 Reduce oven to 160°C/140°C fan forced. Pour lemon mixture into the cooled pastry case. Bake for 1 hour or until just set. Cool to room temperature, then chill in the fridge for 2 hours.

6 For the meringue, stir the sugar and 60ml (¼ cup) water in a saucepan over low heat until the sugar dissolves, brushing down the side of the pan with a wet pastry brush. Cook the sugar syrup, without stirring, over medium-high heat for 3-5 minutes or until it reaches 115°C (soft ball stage) on a cook's thermometer.

7 While the syrup continues to cook, use an electric mixer with a whisk attachment to whisk the egg whites and cream of tartar until soft peaks form.

8 When the syrup reaches 121°C (hard ball stage), slowly pour it into the egg white mixture. Whisk on high speed until the meringue is thick and glossy.

9 Place the chilled lemon pie on a serving plate. Spoon the meringue onto the pie. Use a flat-bladed knife to make swirls and peaks in the meringue. Use a kitchen blowtorch to caramelise the meringue. Serve.

○ GLUTEN FREE　● MAKE AHEAD　○ FREEZABLE　● KID FRIENDLY　○ EASY

★★★★★ *This was beautiful. I had never made Italian meringue before — I don't have a cook's thermometer and it still worked out really well. Go for it, I say! It was heaven.*

ANGEANDDAVE

STEP-BY-STEP
HOW-TO GUIDE

Master the art of fluffy Italian meringue with these easy steps.

1 Italian meringue is made with a hot sugar syrup, so it doesn't require further cooking. When making the syrup, it's important to brush the side of the pan with a wet pastry brush to prevent sugar crystals forming.

2 It's essential to cook the sugar syrup to the correct temperature. 'Soft ball stage' means that if you dropped a little into cold water, it would form a soft ball. For 'hard ball stage', it would form a firm ball.

3 Make sure your mixer bowl and whisk are completely dry and clean before mixing the egg whites, otherwise the mixture might not form peaks. Adding cream of tartar helps the mixture to stabilise.

4 Keep the motor running on the mixer while you slowly and steadily pour in the sugar syrup. This helps the syrup to be thoroughly incorporated. Keep mixing until the meringue is thick and cooled to room temperature.

5 Place the pie on your serving plate or cake stand and use a large spoon to dollop the meringue over the top. Next use a palette knife or the back straight edge of a butter knife to make swirls and peaks in the meringue.

6 A kitchen blowtorch is ideal for quickly and easily caramelising the meringue, but if you don't have one, place the pie on a baking tray and bake at 200°C/180°C fan forced for 5 minutes or until browned.

★★★★★ *It must be good. I made the pie in the afternoon and my son had eaten the whole thing by morning. Oh, to be young and thin again.* **DOGGUSS123**

CLASSIC LEMON SOUFFLÉ

This dessert is easier than you may think, and only needs a few ingredients – the key is in the aeration, and gently mixing the batter to keep it fluffy.

SERVES 4 **PREP** 20 mins **COOK** 25 mins

25g butter, plus extra melted butter, to grease
Caster sugar, to dust
2 tbs plain flour
1 tbs cornflour
250ml (1 cup) milk
70g (⅓ cup) caster sugar
2 tbs lemon juice
1 tbs finely grated lemon rind
4 eggs, at room temperature, separated
Icing sugar, to dust

1 Preheat oven to 200°C/180°C fan forced. Place a baking tray in the oven. Grease four 250ml (1 cup) ovenproof soufflé dishes with extra melted butter and lightly dust with caster sugar.

2 Melt the butter in a saucepan over medium heat until foaming. Add the flour and cornflour. Cook, stirring, for 1 minute or until mixture begins to foam. Remove from the heat. Gradually pour in half the milk, whisking constantly with a balloon whisk until smooth. Gradually add the remaining milk, whisking until smooth and combined. Stir in 55g (¼ cup) sugar.

3 Place saucepan over medium heat and bring to the boil, stirring constantly with a wooden spoon, for 3-4 minutes or until mixture boils and thickens. Remove from the heat and stir in the lemon juice and rind until well combined. Whisk in the yolks. Transfer mixture to a large bowl.

4 Use electric beaters to beat the egg whites in a separate clean, dry bowl until firm peaks form. Gradually add the remaining sugar and whisk until thick and glossy.

5 Add one-quarter of the egg white mixture to the lemon mixture. Use a large metal spoon to fold together until just combined. Add the remaining egg white mixture. Fold together until just combined.

6 Spoon into prepared dishes. Run your finger around the inside rim of each dish. Place dishes on preheated tray. Bake for 20 minutes or until soufflés are puffed and just set. Dust with icing sugar. Serve immediately.

COOK'S TIP

Timing is particularly important for soufflés, so have all your ingredients measured before you start.

○ GLUTEN FREE ○ MAKE AHEAD ○ FREEZABLE ● KID FRIENDLY ○ EASY

★★★★★ When I saw this I realised I already had all the ingredients in the pantry, so I tried it, and it worked perfectly! FOODSLED

STEP-BY-STEP HOW-TO GUIDE

Not sure where to start with making a soufflé? This is the place!

1 Grease the soufflé dishes or straight-sided ramekins all the way to the lip of the dish, then add caster sugar and roll around the dish to make sure it is coated, shaking out any excess. This will help your soufflés rise.

2 When mixing the flours into the melted butter, you want the mixture to form a smooth paste before slowly adding the milk and whisking constantly so it keeps a smooth consistency and doesn't stick to the pan.

3 After finishing the sauce, it's important to transfer it to a bowl before you start whipping the egg whites, so it can cool down. If it's too hot, it may cause your soufflé mixture to collapse.

4 Chilled egg whites don't whip very well, so bring your eggs to room temperature before starting. Also make sure your mixer bowl and whisk are completely dry and clean, otherwise the mixture might not form peaks.

5 When adding the egg whites to the sauce, you want to keep as much air as possible in the mixture. Use a large dry metal spoon to very gently fold together in batches until just combined with no streaks of egg white.

6 After spooning the mixture into the prepared dishes gently push it down to make sure there are no gaps, then run your finger gently around the inside rim of each dish. This helps the soufflé to rise straight with a lovely cap.

★★★★★ *First attempt at making a soufflé and it was a success! They were light and fluffy and looked just like the photo on the recipe.* **LAGUDA76**

VANILLA BEAN CRÈME BRÛLÉE

If this devilishly delicious dessert seems strictly chefs only, think again! There are just two techniques to master – both of which are simple using our guide.

SERVES 4 **PREP** 15 mins (+ cooling & 4 hours chilling) **COOK** 40 mins

300ml pouring cream
250ml (1 cup) milk
1 vanilla bean, split
5 egg yolks
70g (⅓ cup) caster sugar
1 tbs raw caster sugar

1 Preheat oven to 150°C/130°C fan forced. Place the cream and milk in a saucepan over medium heat. Scrape the seeds from the vanilla bean pod into the cream mixture, add the bean and bring almost to the boil.

2 Meanwhile, whisk the egg yolks and caster sugar in a large heatproof bowl until well combined.

3 Whisk the cream mixture into the egg mixture. Strain into a jug, discarding vanilla bean pod. Place four 185ml ovenproof ramekins in a roasting pan and divide mixture among ramekins. Add boiling water to the roasting pan to reach halfway up the sides of the ramekins. Bake for 35 minutes or until just set.

4 Remove ramekins from the roasting pan and set aside to cool slightly. Cover and place in fridge for 4 hours or until set. Sprinkle raw sugar over custards. Caramelise with a kitchen blowtorch. Serve.

COOK'S TIP

You can make the custard up to 1 day ahead. Just cover and place in the fridge after baking, then finish with caramelised sugar just before serving.

★★★★★ *Yum! This is a winner and have made it so many times for friends. Rich, smooth and one of the best brûlée recipes. Follow the easy directions and it has been foolproof so far.* **LIBSTERM**

● GLUTEN FREE ● MAKE AHEAD ○ FREEZABLE ○ KID FRIENDLY ○ EASY

HOW-TO GUIDE

Silky custard and a crackingly good topping are just a few steps away.

1 Use a small sharp knife to scrape the seeds from the vanilla bean pod. If you don't have vanilla beans, you could use 1 tsp vanilla bean paste instead. Add both the bean and the seeds to the cream mixture.

2 Heat the cream, milk and vanilla bean and seeds gently over medium heat so the mixture has time to infuse with the vanilla flavour. Don't let it boil – you want to bring it to a very gentle simmer.

3 You can use a hand-held balloon whisk or electric beaters to beat the egg yolks and sugar together. Beat until the mixture is smooth with no grains of sugar and has turned a pale yellow colour.

4 After whisking the cream mixture into the egg mixture, pour through a sieve into a heatproof jug – this will ensure your custard mixture is perfectly smooth and also makes it easier to pour into the ramekins.

5 Pouring the water into the roasting pan to come halfway up the sides of the ramekins acts as a water bath that will make the custard gently set. Be careful not to let any water into the ramekins or the custard will stay runny.

6 A kitchen blowtorch is ideal for caramelising the sugar, but if you don't have one, place the ramekins on a baking tray under the hot grill about 6cm away from the heat for 2 to 3 minutes or until caramelised.

TWIST IT!

To make a Chocolate crème brûlée, add 150g finely chopped dark chocolate at the end of Step 1.

TWIST IT!

To make a Coffee crème brûlée, replace the vanilla bean with 1 tbs instant coffee and whisk 2 tbs Kahlua liqueur with the egg yolks and sugar.

CHOCOLATE LAVA PUDDINGS

Wow the crowd with this indulgent dinner party favourite, plus
a beautifully glossy homemade raspberry sorbet.

MAKES 6 **PREP** 20 mins (+ 8 hours chilling) **COOK** 20 mins

200g dark chocolate (70% cocoa),
  finely chopped
200g unsalted butter, chopped,
  plus extra, to grease
Cocoa powder, to dust
4 eggs
4 egg yolks
100g (½ cup) caster sugar
50g (⅓ cup) plain flour
1½ tbs cocoa powder, extra

RASPBERRY SORBET
600g frozen raspberries, thawed
215g (1 cup) caster sugar
100ml water
1½ tsp lemon juice
1 egg white, lightly whisked
  with a fork

1 For the sorbet, process berries in a food processor until
smooth. Strain through a fine sieve into a bowl, pushing
mixture through with the back of a spoon. Discard seeds.

2 Place sugar and water in a saucepan over medium heat.
Cook, stirring, for 3 minutes or until sugar dissolves.
Bring to the boil. Simmer for 2 minutes or until thickened.
Set aside to cool. Stir syrup and lemon juice into raspberry
puree. Pour into a tray. Freeze for 2 hours until almost frozen.

3 Use a spoon to break up frozen puree. Process until just
smooth. With the motor running, slowly add the egg
white until combined and glossy. Spoon into an airtight
container and freeze for 6-8 hours or until set.

4 Place the chocolate and butter in a heatproof bowl set
over a saucepan of simmering water (don't let the bowl
touch the water). Cook, stirring with a metal spoon, until
smooth. Set aside to cool slightly. Lightly grease six 180ml
dariole moulds with butter. Dust lightly with cocoa.

5 Use a balloon whisk to whisk the eggs, yolks and sugar
in a bowl until sugar dissolves. Stir in the chocolate
mixture. Sift over flour and cocoa. Fold until combined.
Divide among moulds, filling to three-quarters full. Place
in the fridge, uncovered, for 1-2 hours or until chilled.

6 Preheat oven to 220°C/200°C fan forced. Place
puddings on a baking tray. Bake for 12 minutes or until
puffed and just set (centre should wobble slightly). Stand for
1 minute. Carefully turn puddings onto serving plates. Dust
with cocoa. Serve with scoops of sorbet.

COOK'S TIP

Make the
puddings to the
end of Step 5.
Store, uncovered,
in the fridge for
up to 8 hours,
then continue
with the recipe
when ready.

○ GLUTEN FREE ● MAKE AHEAD ○ FREEZABLE ○ KID FRIENDLY ○ EASY

20 *minutes prep*

STEP-BY-STEP
HOW-TO GUIDE

Love to get these lava puddings and sorbet perfect? Here's how!

1 For a lovely smooth sorbet, whiz the berries in a food processor, then strain through a fine sieve into a large bowl, pressing with the back of a spoon to make sure you extract as much juice as possible.

2 After stirring the cooled syrup and juice into the raspberry puree, pour the mixture into a large tray with sides. You want a large surface area so the sorbet freezes evenly, but check first to make sure your tray will fit in the freezer!

3 Adding the egg white helps to stabilise the sorbet mixture and make it a little bit creamy. To make the finished result even more glossy and smooth, process the mixture again after freezing for the second time.

4 Lightly grease the inside of your dariole moulds with butter, then add cocoa and roll around the mould to make sure it is coated, shaking out any excess. This will prevent your puddings sticking when you turn them out.

5 When adding the flour and cocoa, sift it over the chocolate mixture, then fold gently until combined. This will help to ensure your pudding mixture is light and airy. The puddings will rise, so only fill the moulds three-quarters full.

6 Place the puddings on a baking tray so they're easy to put into and remove from the oven. Baking them until they're only just set with a slight wobble is what will make them have a rich and runny 'lava' centre.

★★★★★

Wow! My 13-year-old requested these for his birthday dessert and they were fantastic – he was so chuffed. The chocolate filling oozed out of them, just like the picture!

WAFFLEISO

RASPBERRY & CUSTARD TART

Filled with sweet crème pâtissière and topped with glistening fresh raspberries, this pretty tart is the pièce de résistance.

SERVES 6 **PREP** 40 mins (+ cooling & 4 hours chilling) **COOK** 25 mins

1 vanilla bean, split
500ml (2 cups) milk
100g (½ cup) caster sugar
7 egg yolks
35g (¼ cup) cornflour
225g (1½ cups) plain flour
2 tbs icing sugar
125g chilled butter, chopped
2 tbs cold water
1 egg white, lightly whisked
60ml (¼ cup) thickened cream, whipped
3 x 125g punnets fresh raspberries
90g (¼ cup) raspberry jam, warmed
1 tbs amaretto liqueur (optional)

1 Reserve half the vanilla bean. Place the milk in a saucepan. Add the remaining vanilla bean half, scraping in the seeds. Bring to boil, stirring.

2 Use electric beaters to beat the sugar and 6 egg yolks in a bowl until pale and creamy. Gradually beat in the cornflour, then the milk mixture, with the motor running. Strain into a clean saucepan over medium-low heat. Stir for 1 minute or until thick. Transfer to a bowl. Cool slightly. Cover surface with plastic wrap. Place in fridge for 4 hours to chill.

3 Meanwhile, process flour and icing sugar in a food processor until just combined. Add butter and seeds from reserved vanilla bean. Process until mixture resembles fine crumbs. Add remaining egg yolk and water. Process until dough just comes together. Turn onto a lightly floured surface. Knead until smooth. Shape into a disc. Cover. Place in the fridge for 1 hour to rest.

4 Roll out pastry on a floured surface until 5mm thick. Line a 19 x 27cm (base measurement) fluted tart tin, with removable base, with pastry. Trim excess. Place in fridge for 1 hour to rest.

5 Preheat oven to 200°C. Use a fork to prick the pastry base all over. Line with baking paper and fill with pastry weights or uncooked rice. Bake for 12-15 minutes. Remove paper and weights. Bake for a further 5 minutes or until light golden. Lightly brush with egg white. Set aside in tin on a wire rack to cool completely.

6 Fold the cream into the custard. Spoon into the pastry case and smooth the surface. Top with the raspberries. Combine jam and amaretto in a bowl. Strain through a sieve. Discard seeds. Brush jam mixture over the raspberries.

COOK'S TIP

You can use other berries such as blueberries, blackberries or small strawberries if you like.

○ GLUTEN FREE ● **MAKE AHEAD** ○ FREEZABLE ● **KID FRIENDLY** ○ EASY

STEP-BY-STEP HOW TO GUIDE

These tips will help you achieve a dreamy custard and gorgeous presentation.

1 To avoid scrambling the egg for the custard, slowly pour In the hot milk with the motor running.

2 For the perfect crème pâtissière filling, keep cooking and stirring the custard until it's very thick.

3 For uniform presentation, place a line of raspberries at one end and use this as your guide for the rest.

LEMON CURD PUDDING

The super-simple method and dreamy coconut-lemon flavour combo make this a favourite no-fuss dessert. Give it a whirl!

SERVES 8 **PREP** 20 mins (+ cooling) **COOK** 50 mins

4 eggs
250ml (1 cup) coconut milk
100g butter, melted
100g (½ cup) caster sugar
75g (½ cup) plain flour
85g (1 cup) desiccated coconut
600ml double cream
Pure icing sugar, to dust
MICROWAVE LEMON CURD
2 eggs
100g (½ cup) caster sugar
85g butter, melted, cooled
160ml (⅔ cup) fresh lemon juice
2 tsp finely grated lemon rind

1 For the microwave lemon curd, place all the ingredients in a large microwave-safe bowl and whisk to combine. Microwave on Medium, stirring every minute, for 4 minutes or until smooth and thick. Set aside to cool.

2 Preheat oven to 170°C/150°C fan forced. Grease a 23cm (base measurement) round ovenproof dish.

3 Place the eggs, milk, butter, caster sugar, flour and coconut in a large bowl and whisk to combine. Pour mixture into the prepared dish.

4 Remove ¼ cupful of the lemon curd and use to dollop teaspoonfuls of curd randomly on top of the pie mixture. Use a bamboo or metal skewer to lightly swirl the curd dollops to create a slight marble effect in the pie mixture.

5 Bake for 45 minutes or until a skewer inserted into the centre of the pudding comes out clean. Set aside for 10 minutes to cool slightly.

6 Use a balloon whisk to whisk cream in a bowl until soft peaks form. Fold in the remaining curd to create a ripple effect. Dollop onto the pudding and dust with icing sugar.

COOK'S TIP

The lemon curd is ready when it's thick enough to coat the back of a wooden spoon.

★★★★★ *I've always made lemon curd on the stovetop, but I'll be making it in the microwave from now on! Such an easy dessert.* **BAKINGSELFIES**

○ GLUTEN FREE ○ MAKE AHEAD ○ FREEZABLE ● KID FRIENDLY ● EASY

STEP-BY-STEP HOW TO GUIDE
You don't need any fancy equipment to make this amazing pudding!

1 Gently swirling the curd will help to lightly distribute it throughout the pudding and create a marbled effect.

2 When testing to see if the pudding is cooked, insert the skewer into a section with cake, not curd.

3 Use a large spoon to gently fold the curd into the whisked cream, keeping as much airiness as possible.

RICH CHOCOLATE BROWNIES

Take your brownies to the next level with our classic rich chocolate recipe – or try your hand at one of our variations!

MAKES 18 **PREP** 15 mins (+ overnight cooling) **COOK** 45 mins

200g dark cooking chocolate,
  coarsely chopped
150g butter, chopped
3 eggs, lightly whisked
215g (1 cup) caster sugar
115g (¾ cup) plain flour
35g (⅓ cup) cocoa powder

1 Preheat oven to 160°C/140°C fan forced. Grease a 16 x 26cm slice pan and line with non-stick baking paper, allowing the sides to overhang.

2 Melt the chocolate and butter in a heatproof bowl over a saucepan half-filled with simmering water (don't let the water touch the bowl), stirring occasionally until smooth. Set aside for 5 minutes to cool.

3 Stir the whisked egg into the chocolate mixture. Sift the sugar, flour and cocoa powder into the mixture, and stir until just combined.

4 Pour mixture into the prepared pan. Use the back of a spoon to spread the mixture into the corners of the pan and smooth the surface.

5 Bake for 40 minutes or until crumbs cling to a skewer inserted into the centre. Set aside in the pan for 6 hours or overnight to cool. Serve.

COOK'S TIP

To freeze these brownies, wrap cooled uncut brownies in 2 layers of foil and 1 layer of plastic wrap. Freeze for up to 4 months.

★★★★★ *I made this with my friend and they are amazing! Super easy, will be making again. This ones going in the recipe book!* **IZABEL.T**

○ GLUTEN FREE ● MAKE AHEAD ● FREEZABLE ○ KID FRIENDLY ● EASY

STEP-BY-STEP

HOW-TO GUIDE

Making amazing brownies is easy with our handy tips.

1 Lining your baking tin with the edges overhanging will help you to lift the brownie out of the pan. Use scissors to cut the paper to the correct size so that the corners sit neatly and grease the pan first to help the paper sit in place.

2 When melting chocolate, the water should be just simmering, not boiling. The bowl and spoon need to be completely dry before you start, otherwise the chocolate may seize and become grainy.

3 Use a plastic spatula or large spoon to gently stir the egg into the chocolate mixture, then fold in the remaining ingredients until just combined – this will help create the lovely fudgy texture.

4 The brownie mixture is quite thick, so after pouring it into the prepared pan, use the back of a spoon or offset spatula to spread the mixture into the corners of the pan and smooth the surface so it is level.

5 The texture of this brownie is fudgy and sticky, so to test if it's ready, a skewer inserted should come out with a few crumbs clinging. Allow the brownie to cool completely in the pan – it will continue to set as it cools.

6 These brownies taste better the next day, so if you have time, after they've cooled completely, remove from the pan and place, uncut, in an airtight container overnight. Cut into 18 slices to serve.

TWIST IT!

Take your brownies to the next level by adding chunky pieces of your favourite choccy bar. For mint brownies, stir 5 x 40g Aero peppermint bars, divided into squares, into the brownie mixture at the end of Step 3. For Cherry Ripe brownies, stir 4 x 52g Cherry Ripe bars, cut into 1.5cm pieces, into the brownie mixture at the end of Step 3. For Malteser brownies, stir 200g Maltesers into the brownie mixture at the end of Step 3.

MAPLE-SPICED PECAN PIE

Give this classic pecan pie a little extra flair with beautiful golden pastry leaves and a super-easy spiced rum ice-cream.

SERVES 8 **PREP** 20 mins (+ chilling & 6 hours freezing) **COOK** 50 mins

3 eggs, lightly whisked
125ml (½ cup) maple syrup
100g (½ cup, firmly packed) brown
    sugar
50g butter, melted
½ tsp vanilla bean paste
300g pecan halves

SPICED RUM ICE-CREAM
1.5L vanilla ice-cream,
    softened
40ml (¼ cup) spiced rum
½ tsp ground cinnamon

PASTRY
225g (1½ cups) plain flour
2 tbs icing sugar mixture
150g chilled butter, chopped
1 egg yolk
2 tbs chilled water

1 For the spiced rum ice-cream, place softened ice-cream, spiced rum and cinnamon in a large bowl and stir until well combined. Transfer to a shallow metal container and cover with foil. Place in the freezer for 6 hours or until firm.

2 For the pastry, process the flour, icing sugar and butter in a food processor until it resembles fine crumbs. Add yolk and water. Process until the dough just comes together. Turn onto a lightly floured surface. Knead until smooth. Cover. Place in the fridge for 30 minutes.

3 Preheat oven to 200°C/180°C fan forced. Roll out dough between 2 sheets of baking paper to a 4mm-thick disc. Line a 3cm-deep, 26cm (top measurement) fluted tart tin with removable base, with pastry. Trim and reserve excess. Place in the fridge for 15 minutes, to rest.

4 Cover pastry base with baking paper and fill with pastry weights or uncooked rice. Bake for 15 minutes. Remove the paper and weights. Bake for a further 10 minutes or until crisp and golden.

5 Reduce oven temperature to 180°C/160°C fan forced. Whisk the egg, maple syrup, sugar, butter and vanilla in a bowl. Stir in the pecans. Pour evenly into the pastry base. Bake for 25 minutes or until set. Set aside for 1 hour to cool. Decorate with pastry leaves (see tip). Serve topped with spiced rum ice-cream.

COOK'S TIP

To make the pastry leaves, cut leaf shapes from scraps. Brush with egg wash and bake on a lined tray until golden.

○ GLUTEN FREE   ● MAKE AHEAD   ○ FREEZABLE   ○ KID FRIENDLY   ○ EASY

STEP-BY-STEP HOW TO GUIDE

Learn the secrets to our cheat's ice-cream, plus how to make the perfect pastry shell!

1 When mixing the ice-cream, you want it to be softened, but not runny. Use a large spoon to evenly combine.

2 Use your rolling pin to lift and gently lower the pastry into the tin, then use your fingers to fit into the edges.

3 Blind baking with weights or uncooked rice stops the pastry from puffing up or over-browning.

CLASSIC CHOCOLATE ÉCLAIRS

Crisp golden choux pastry filled with rich vanilla bean custard and drizzled with glossy chocolate icing… what's not to love?

MAKES 18-20 **PREP** 30 mins (+ cooling) **COOK** 40 mins

125ml (½ cup) water
125ml (½ cup) milk
80g butter, at room temperature, chopped
150g (1 cup) plain flour
3 eggs, at room temperature
330g pkt royal icing
2 tbs cocoa powder
2 tsp water, extra

CRÈME PÂTISSIÈRE
375ml (1½ cups) milk
1 tsp vanilla bean paste
3 egg yolks
70g (⅓ cup) caster sugar
50g (⅓ cup) plain flour

1 For the crème pâtissière, warm the milk and vanilla in a saucepan over low heat. Whisk the yolks and sugar in a bowl until thick. Whisk in the flour, then milk mixture. Return to the pan over low heat and cook, whisking, for 5 minutes or until thickened. Transfer to a bowl and cover the surface with plastic wrap. Set aside.

2 Place the water, milk and butter in a saucepan over high heat and bring just to the boil. Remove from the heat. Use a wooden spoon to beat in the flour until combined. Cook, stirring, over medium heat for 2-3 minutes or until mixture forms a ball and comes away from the side of the pan. Set aside for 5 minutes to cool.

3 Use electric beaters to gradually beat the eggs, 1 at a time, into the flour mixture, beating well after each addition, until the dough is thick and glossy.

4 Preheat oven to 180°C/160°C fan forced and line 2 baking trays with baking paper. Spoon the dough into a piping bag fitted with a 1.5cm round nozzle and pipe eighteen 11cm logs onto the prepared trays. Sprinkle with water to create steam. Bake for 25 minutes or until puffed and golden. Turn éclairs over. Cut a slit in bases. Bake for 5-10 minutes. Transfer to a wire rack to cool.

5 Spoon crème pâtissière into a piping bag fitted with a 5mm nozzle. Push nozzle into an éclair and fill with crème. Repeat with remaining éclairs.

6 Prepare royal icing following packet directions. Spoon ¼ cup icing into a piping bag fitted with a 2mm round nozzle. Stir cocoa and extra water together in a bowl. Add to the remaining icing mixture and stir. Spread an éclair with chocolate icing. Pipe a zigzag pattern on top with the white icing. Use a skewer to drag white icing through the chocolate icing. Repeat with remaining éclairs and icing. Set aside for 10 minutes. Serve.

○ GLUTEN FREE ○ MAKE AHEAD ○ FREEZABLE ● **KID FRIENDLY** ○ EASY

★ ★ ★ ★ ★ *These were fantastic. I loved the trick with the zigzag icing – they looked very flash.* **DRPRETTY**

STEP-BY-STEP
HOW-TO GUIDE

Wow the crowd with perfect choux pastry and a luxe custard filling.

1 Crème pâtissière means 'pastry cream' and is a custard that is thickened with flour, making it perfect for filling éclairs. Cover the surface with plastic wrap to prevent a skin forming and allow to cool completely.

2 Have everything measured and ready before making the choux pastry for your éclairs, so you can pay full attention to the cooking process. Cook until the dough comes away from the side of the pan and forms a ball.

3 Allow the mixture to cool for the full 5 minutes so the eggs don't cook when they are added in. Make sure the eggs are at room temperature – this will help the dough to rise and have a lovely puffy texture.

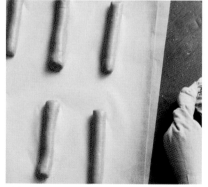

4 When piping the dough onto the lined trays, make sure there is enough space between them to expand and rise. Keep the pressure on the piping bag steady, so the eclairs are the same thickness along the whole length.

5 Cutting a slit in the eclairs before they finish baking dries out the inside, so they won't be soggy when you fill them. When filling the eclairs, tilt the nozzle of the piping bag gently each way to evenly fill with crème.

6 This beautiful bakery-style icing is really simple to achieve. Place the eclairs on a wire rack set over a tray to catch any drips. Try dragging the skewer in different directions to make different patterns.

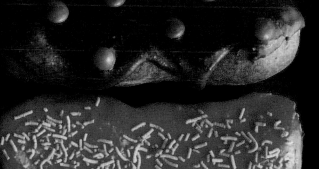

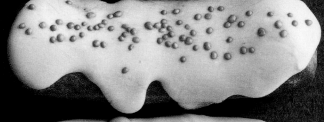

TWIST IT! Have fun! Make the eclair cases and fill with crème pâtissière. Divide icing into multiple bowls. Add food colouring to each and ice the eclairs with different colours. Decorate with choc minis, sprinkles or cachous.

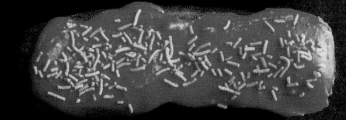

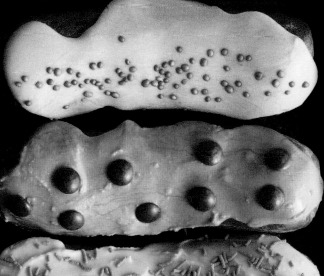

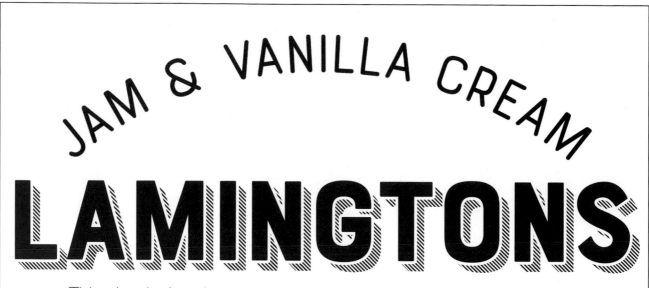

JAM & VANILLA CREAM LAMINGTONS

This classic Aussie treat is always a crowd pleaser. We've tricked these up with jam and cream to make them extra special.

MAKES 15 **PREP** 30 mins (+ cooling, chilling & setting) **COOK** 40 mins

250g butter, at room temperature, chopped
215g (1 cup) caster sugar
3 eggs
2 tsp vanilla extract
300g (2 cups) self-raising flour
125ml (½ cup) milk
170g (2 cups) desiccated coconut
300ml ctn thickened cream
½ tsp vanilla bean paste
245g (¾ cup) strawberry jam

CHOCOLATE COATING
450g (3 cups) icing sugar mixture
2 tbs dark Dutch cocoa
30g butter, chopped
185ml (¾ cup) boiling water

1 Preheat oven to 180°C/160°C fan forced. Line base and sides of a 20 x 30cm slice pan with baking paper.

2 Use electric beaters to beat butter and sugar in a bowl until pale and creamy. Beat in the eggs, 1 at a time, beating well after each addition. Beat in vanilla extract. Fold in the flour and milk until well combined. Pour into the prepared pan and smooth the top. Bake for 35-40 minutes or until a skewer comes out clean. Cool in the pan for 10 minutes. Transfer to a wire rack to cool.

3 Trim cake edges. Cut into 15 squares. Set a wire rack over a tray. Place coconut on a plate.

4 For the chocolate coating, place the icing sugar, cocoa and butter in a heatproof bowl. Pour over boiling water. Stir until melted and combined.

5 Place a cake square in the chocolate coating. Use 2 forks to turn to coat. Remove and allow excess coating to drain off. Roll in coconut to coat. Place on wire rack for 30 minutes to set. Repeat with remaining cake squares, chocolate coating and coconut.

6 Use electric beaters with the whisk attachment to whisk cream and vanilla bean paste in a bowl until firm peaks form. Spoon into a piping bag fitted with a 1cm star nozzle. Use a serrated knife to cut the lamingtons horizontally.

7 Spread 2 tsp jam on 1 cut side of lamington. Pipe cream on top. Top with remaining lamington half. Place carefully on a tray. Repeat with remaining lamingtons, jam and cream. Place tray in the fridge for 30 minutes, to set the cream. Serve.

COOK'S TIP

You can make unfilled lamingtons to the end of Step 4 up to 4 days ahead. Store in an airtight container in a cool dark place. Cut and fill before serving.

○ GLUTEN FREE   ● MAKE AHEAD   ○ FREEZABLE   ● KID FRIENDLY   ○ EASY

★★★★★ *Loved these! I didn't have a piping bag, so I put the cream in a plastic bag and snipped the corner off. They still looked great!* **FRIDGETUNER**

STEP-BY-STEP
HOW-TO GUIDE

Here's all the tricks you need for the perfect lamingtons.

1 For perfectly light textured butter cake, beat the butter and sugar until very light in colour. This ensures that you'll end up with as much aeration as possible.

2 A skewer should come out clean when the cake is ready. Trimming the edges of the cake after it has cooled allows all the sides to evenly absorb the chocolate coating.

3 The chocolate coating is thinner than a standard icing, so don't worry if it looks runny. This allows it to be absorbed by the cake more easily. Stir until smooth and combined.

4 Be careful – don't oversoak the lamingtons in the chocolate coating, as the cake with continue to absorb the liquid, making the lamingtons soggy.

5 Use a gentle sawing action to evenly cut the lamingtons. Cut them so the base is about two-thirds up the side, so the weight of the top doesn't make the cream ooze out.

6 Once filled with jam and cream, keep the lamingtons in the fridge. Remove from the fridge 20-30 minutes before serving for a softer, more flavoursome cake.

BRIOCHE BREAD & BUTTER PUDDING

Everyone needs a comforting pud in their repertoire. Buttery brioche laden with rich custard will keep the gang happy.

SERVES 8 **PREP** 15 mins (+ soaking) **COOK** 45 mins

400g pkt butter brioche loaf
100g dark chocolate (70% cocoa), coarsely chopped
2 x 395g cans sweetened condensed milk
500ml (2 cups) pouring cream
8 eggs
2 tsp vanilla extract

BURNT CARAMEL SAUCE
100g (½ cup) caster sugar
80ml (⅓ cup) double cream

1 Preheat oven to 180°C/160°C fan forced. Grease a round 3L ovenproof dish. Trim ends of the brioche then use a serrated bread knife to cut into 1cm-thick slices.

2 Place the slices in the prepared dish, overlapping in a concentric circle pattern and sprinkling three-quarters of the chocolate between the layers as you go.

3 Whisk together condensed milk, cream, eggs and vanilla in a large bowl. Pour mixture through a fine sieve over the bread slices and set aside for 30 minutes to soak.

4 Sprinkle the remaining chopped dark chocolate over the brioche. Bake for 45 minutes or until set and golden.

5 Meanwhile, for the burnt caramel sauce, stir the sugar and 60ml (¼ cup) water in a saucepan over low heat for 5 minutes or until sugar dissolves. Bring to the boil and cook, without stirring, for 5 minutes or until deep golden. Remove from the heat. Carefully stir in the double cream (mixture may spit). Set aside for 15 minutes to cool and thicken slightly. Drizzle over the pudding to serve.

COOK'S TIP

You can use panettone instead of the brioche, if you prefer.

★★★★★ *Made this for pudding after a Sunday roast. I loved the fan effect from layering the brioche that way.* **DRAGONRIDER**

○ GLUTEN FREE ○ MAKE AHEAD ○ FREEZABLE ● KID FRIENDLY ● EASY

STEP-BY-STEP HOW TO GUIDE

Take your bread and butter pudding game to the next level.

1 Arrange the brioche to create a spiral pattern. Don't worry about any gaps, as they will be filled by the custard.

2 The burnt caramel sauce is cooked for longer than a standard caramel, until just before it burns.

3 Be careful when stirring the cream into the caramel. Wear oven mitts if you like, as the mixture may spit.

RHUBARB & GINGER CRUMBLE

A crumble is basically a crunchy topping with sweet and juicy fruit beneath.
Master the basic techniques with this biscuit-laced version.

SERVES 4 **PREP** 20 mins **COOK** 35 mins

1 bunch (about 7 stems) rhubarb
2 tbs white sugar
1 tbs finely chopped glacé ginger
Vanilla ice-cream, to serve
BISCUIT CRUMBLE TOPPING
115g (¾ cup) plain flour
100g butter, chilled,
   chopped
100g (½ cup, firmly packed)
   brown sugar
100g Anzac biscuits, coarsely
   chopped

1 Preheat the oven to 180°C/160°C fan forced. Remove the leaves from the rhubarb and discard. Wash the stems and trim the ends. Cut stems into 1.5cm lengths.

2 Place the rhubarb, sugar and glacé ginger in a large bowl. Use a wooden spoon to stir until well combined and the rhubarb is evenly coated in the sugar.

3 For the biscuit crumble topping, place the flour in a large bowl. Use your fingertips to rub in butter until mixture resembles coarse crumbs. Stir in the sugar and chopped biscuit.

4 Divide filling among six 250ml (1 cup) ovenproof dishes. Spoon the topping evenly over the rhubarb mixture.

5 Bake the crumbles for 30-35 minutes or until the topping is golden and rhubarb is tender. Serve with ice-cream.

COOK'S TIP

Apples, pears, berries and stone fruit all work with crumbles. Try different spices for flavour twists.

○ GLUTEN FREE ○ MAKE AHEAD ○ FREEZABLE ● KID FRIENDLY ● EASY

20 *minutes prep*

★★★★★ *Beautiful! I used stem ginger biscuits instead of Anzacs and crystallised ginger in place of glacé, and it was delicious!* **AMALFIAMY**

STEP-BY-STEP
HOW-TO GUIDE

Once you know how, fruit crumble will be a regular on your menu!

1 Remove and discard the leaves from the rhubarb before cutting into pieces, as the leaves are poisonous. Cut stems into 1.5cm lengths to ensure the rhubarb cooks evenly.

2 Rhubarb is quite tart, so make sure to stir with a wooden spoon to coat evenly in the sugar, as this will sweeten it. You can swap the ginger for orange zest, if you prefer.

3 It's important for the butter to be chilled and to use your fingertips to rub it into the flour. Don't use your palms, as the butter can melt and make the topping cakey.

4 Leave enough room at the top of each dish for the crumble topping. If you don't have individual dishes, you can cook the crumble in one 1.5L (6 cup) ovenproof dish instead.

5 When sprinkling the crumble topping over the rhubarb, make sure it is evenly distributed, but you can leave some gaps around the edge if you like, so the juices bubble up the sides.

6 To test if the rhubarb is tender, insert a small sharp knife through the crumble and into the rhubarb. It should insert easily. Stand the crumbles for 5 minutes before serving.

HAZELNUT & LEMON VACHERIN

We've used citrus and rich hazelnuts in our version of this French work of art. Make the elements ahead of time, ready to assemble and serve.

SERVES 8 **PREP** 35 mins (+ chilling & cooling) **COOK** 40 mins

285g (1⅓ cups) caster sugar
4 eggs, separated
125ml (½ cup) milk
60ml (¼ cup) lemon juice
1 tbs finely grated lemon rind
2 tsp cornflour
30g butter, chopped
1 tsp vanilla bean paste
55g (½ cup) hazelnut meal
600ml ctn thickened cream, whipped
55g (⅓ cup) hazelnuts, toasted, chopped

1 Preheat oven to 160°C. Line a 35 x 25cm (base measurement) slice pan with baking paper.

2 Combine 215g (1 cup) sugar, the egg yolks, milk, lemon juice and rind, cornflour and butter in a saucepan over low heat. Cook, whisking, for 3-5 minutes or until mixture boils and thickens. Transfer to a bowl. Cover the surface with plastic wrap and chill in the fridge for 30 minutes.

3 Meanwhile, use electric beaters to beat the egg whites, vanilla and remaining sugar in a bowl until thick and glossy. Fold in the hazelnut meal. Spoon into the prepared pan and spread to the edges. Bake for 30-35 minutes or until firm. Cool in the pan for 15 minutes.

4 Turn the meringue out onto a piece of baking paper. Cut crossways into 4 rectangles. Place 1 rectangle on a plate. Spread with one-third of the lemon mixture. Top with one-quarter of the whipped cream. Repeat layers twice. Top with the remaining meringue and remaining cream, and sprinkle with hazelnuts to serve.

COOK'S TIP

Make the meringue and lemon mixture up to 6 hours ahead. Stir lemon mixture before spreading. Once assembled, store in the fridge for up to an hour.

★★★★★ *Easy to make especially the lemon curd. Looks like the picture, cuts really well, looks very impressive.* **BOMBAZEEN**

○ GLUTEN FREE ● MAKE AHEAD ○ FREEZABLE ○ KID FRIENDLY ○ EASY

STEP-BY-STEP HOW TO GUIDE

Whip up thick, rich lemon curd and the meringue for our patisserie-worthy French vacherin with these top tips.

1 To avoid lumpy lemon curd and scrambling the egg yolk mixture, whisk it constantly over low heat.

2 Cook the lemon curd until it boils and thickens. It's ready when it coats a wooden spoon.

3 Don't worry if the meringue cracks – it'll be layered with curd and cream, so won't affect the overall look.

PERFECT MINI FRUIT PAVLOVAS

Reach the pinnacle of pavlovas – a crispy shell that's chewy inside – in a few simple steps and try our twists on toppers to take it to delicious heights!

SERVES 4 **PREP** 30 mins (+ cooling) **COOK** 1 hour 45 mins

4 egg whites, at room temperature
215g (1 cup) caster sugar
1 tsp white wine vinegar
1 tsp vanilla extract
2 tsp cornflour

CUSTARD CREAM
250ml (1 cup) double thick custard
125ml (½ cup) thickened cream
85g (⅓ cup) double cream

RHUBARB & RASPBERRY TOPPING
1 bunch rhubarb, trimmed, cut into
   6cm lengths
2 tbs caster sugar
125ml (½ cup) fresh orange juice
125g fresh raspberries
2 tbs halved pistachio kernels

1 Preheat oven to 110°C/90°C fan forced. Draw four 10cm circles on a sheet of baking paper and place, ink-side down, on a baking tray.

2 Use electric beaters fitted with the whisk attachment to whisk the egg whites in a clean, dry bowl until firm peaks form. Gradually add the sugar, 1 tbs at a time, beating constantly, until sugar dissolves and mixture is thick and glossy. Quickly beat in the vinegar and vanilla. Beat in the cornflour until just combined.

3 Divide meringue among marked circles on baking paper. Use a knife to spread and shape, roughing up the sides.

4 Bake for 1 hour 30 minutes or until crisp and dry. Turn off oven. Leave pavlovas in oven, with the door closed, to cool completely.

5 For the custard cream, use electric beaters to beat the custard and creams in a bowl until firm peaks form. Place in the fridge until required.

6 Preheat oven to 180°C/160°C fan forced. Place the rhubarb in a roasting pan. Add sugar and orange juice. Toss to combine. Roast for 15 minutes or until rhubarb is tender but still holds its shape. Set aside to cool.

7 Top each pavlova with custard cream, the roasted rhubarb and any syrup from the pan. Scatter over raspberries and pistachio kernels.

COOK'S TIP

If raspberries aren't in season, you can swap them for any other berries.

○ GLUTEN FREE ○ MAKE AHEAD ○ FREEZABLE ● KID FRIENDLY ○ EASY

★★★★★ *I made these the morning of a dinner party and sprinkled over a little grated white chocolate. Everyone loved them!* **DANI.BROUGHAM**

STEP-BY-STEP
HOW-TO GUIDE

Read on to learn the all the secrets you need for pavlova perfection.

1 Use a round cookie cutter, glass or small bowl to outline four 10cm circles on a sheet of baking paper. Place, ink-side down, on a baking tray, so the ink doesn't touch the meringue.

2 Chilled egg whites don't whip very well, so bring your eggs to room temperature before starting. Also make sure your mixer bowl and whisk are completely dry and clean.

3 Keep the motor running on the mixer while you slowly and steadily add the sugar. You want the meringue to be smooth and glossy without any grains of sugar.

4 Adding cornflour helps to stabilise the meringue, but be careful not to overbeat the mixture after adding the cornflour, otherwise the meringue could become too firm.

5 An offset palette knife is the best tool to spread and shape the meringues. Roughing up the sides creates a little crater in the meringue, perfect for holding the toppings.

6 Baking the meringues at a low temperature helps them to dry out and develop a lovely crisp shell. It's essential to let them cook in the oven so they can continue drying out.

SNICKERS CHEESECAKE: Use electric beaters to beat 125ml (½ cup) thickened cream, 125g cream cheese, at room temperature, 1 tbs icing sugar mixture and 1 tbs caramel sauce to firm peaks. Top each pavlova with cream mixture and sliced Snickers. Drizzle over extra caramel sauce.

TWIST IT!

STRAWBERRY CRUMBLE: Combine 250g hulled and halved strawberries, 2 tbs caster sugar and 2 tbs Chambord liqueur. Set aside for 1-2 hours. Top each pavlova with custard cream (see page 68), strawberries and syrup from the bowl. Sprinkle with 2 crumbled Anzac biscuits.

TWIST IT!

MANGO RIPPLE: Use electric beaters to beat 250ml (1 cup) thickened cream and 85g (⅓ cup) double cream in a bowl until firm peaks form. Blend the flesh of half a mango until pureed. Thinly slice the remaining mango half. Fold the mango puree through the whipped cream until swirled. Top each pavlova with the mango cream and sliced mango. Sprinkle with finely grated lime rind and fresh mint leaves.

TWIST IT!

SPIKED CHOCOLATE MUD CAKE

Lots of chocolate, plus a few secret ingredients and our clever step-by-step tips make this the ultimate mud cake, great for serving a crowd.

SERVES 12   **PREP** 30 mins (+ cooling)   **COOK** 1 hour 30 mins

95g (½ cup) pitted prunes
80ml (⅓ cup) port
185ml (¾ cup) water
250g unsalted butter, chopped
180g dark chocolate, chopped
100g dark chocolate (70% cocoa), chopped
315g (1½ cups) caster sugar
2 tsp vanilla extract
3 eggs
50g sour cream
225g (1½ cups) plain flour
2 tbs dark cocoa powder
1 tsp baking powder
½ tsp salt

SOUR CREAM GANACHE
200g dark chocolate
200g sour cream
3 tsp port

1 Preheat oven to 160°C/140°C fan forced. Grease base and side of a 22cm (base measurement) springform pan and line base and side with baking paper.

2 Place the prunes, port and 60ml (¼ cup) water in a small saucepan over medium-low heat and bring to a simmer. Simmer, stirring occasionally, for 10 minutes or until softened. Cool for 15 minutes. Process until smooth.

3 Meanwhile, place butter, dark chocolates, sugar, vanilla and remaining water in a saucepan over low heat. Cook, stirring, for 5 minutes or until melted and smooth. Transfer to a large bowl and set aside to cool for 15 minutes.

4 Place eggs and sour cream in a small bowl and whisk until combined. Use a balloon whisk to stir prune mixture and egg mixture into the chocolate mixture until well combined and glossy.

5 Sift remaining dry ingredients over the chocolate mixture. Mix until combined. Pour into prepared pan. Bake for 1 hour 15 minutes or until a skewer inserted into the centre comes out with moist crumbs clinging. Cool in pan for 2 hours. Transfer to a wire rack to cool completely.

6 Meanwhile, for the sour cream ganache, melt chocolate and cream in a heatproof bowl over a saucepan of simmering water. Remove from the heat. Slowly stir in port. Set aside, stirring occasionally, for 1 hour 30 minutes, until thick. Spread over cake. Serve.

COOK'S TIP

You can make this cake up to 1 day ahead. Store in an airtight container.

○ GLUTEN FREE   ● MAKE AHEAD   ○ FREEZABLE   ○ KID FRIENDLY   ● EASY

STEP-BY-STEP
HOW-TO GUIDE

This pitch-perfect mud cake is easy, with just a few simple steps.

1 Grease the pan well with butter, then use the base of pan to draw a circle on baking paper. Cut out and use to line base of pan. Line the side with a strip of baking paper.

2 The prune mixture adds richness and depth to the cake. After it's cooled for 15 minutes, use a stick blender or small food processor to process well until smooth.

3 After cooking the chocolate mixture until melted and smooth, it's important to transfer it to a bowl to cool for 15 minutes. This makes sure the eggs don't cook when you add them.

4 A balloon whisk is ideal for stirring the prune mixture and egg mixture into the chocolate mixture until combined and glossy, so the mixture has some aeration.

5 Sift the flour, cocoa, baking powder and salt directly over the chocolate mixture, to ensure there are no lumps, then use a large spoon or spatula to mix until combined.

6 When melting the chocolate and cream for the ganache the water in the pan should be just simmering, not boiling. If any water gets into the bowl, the chocolate may become grainy.

★★★★★ This was dense and rich and amazing
— I never would have thought to add prunes!
Perfect for after dinner with coffee. **CURLY_SHIRLEY**

CINNAMON SCROLLS

With melt-in-your mouth pastry and a buttery sweet filling studded with pecans, these iced delights are in a class of their own.

MAKES 9 **PREP** 1 hour (+ cooling, proving, resting & setting) **COOK** 35 mins

265g (1¾ cups) plain flour, plus
  extra, to dust
Pinch of salt
1 tbs caster sugar
2 tsp (7g sachet) dried yeast
1 egg, lightly whisked
160ml (⅔ cup) milk, warmed
Olive oil, to grease
125g butter, chilled,
  cut into 1cm pieces
70g (½ cup) chopped pecans
60ml (¼ cup) honey or golden syrup

FILLING
75g butter, at room temperature
45g (¼ cup, lightly packed)
  brown sugar
2 tbs almond meal
2 tsp ground cinnamon

ICING
80g (½ cup) pure icing sugar, sifted
1 tbs milk
½ tsp vanilla essence

1 Combine flour and salt in a bowl. Make a well in the centre. Add the caster sugar, yeast, egg and milk. Use a flat-bladed knife in a cutting motion to mix until the dough comes together. Turn onto a lightly floured surface and knead until smooth. Brush a large bowl with oil. Place dough in bowl and turn to coat. Cover with plastic wrap. Set aside in a warm, draught-free place for 1 hour or until the dough doubles in size.

2 Punch down the dough with your fist. Turn the dough onto a lightly floured surface. Gently knead until smooth. Roll out the dough to a rectangle about 5mm thick. Top with butter, leaving a 1cm border around the edges. Gently push butter into the dough. Lightly sprinkle with extra flour. Starting at the short end furthest away from you, fold one-third over the centre of the dough. Fold the short side closest to you over the top. Turn the dough 90-degrees clockwise. Gently press the edges together to seal. Use a rolling pin to roll the dough into a rectangle about 5mm thick. Repeat the folding and rolling process 6 times. Cover with plastic wrap and place in the fridge for 30 minutes to rest.

3 To make the filling, use a wooden spoon to beat the butter, brown sugar, almond meal and cinnamon in a medium bowl until smooth and creamy.

4 Line a baking tray with baking paper. On a lightly floured surface, roll pastry into a 32 x 40cm rectangle. Spread evenly with the filling. Top with pecans. Drizzle with honey or golden syrup. Starting from a short end, firmly roll the pastry into a log. Use a knife dusted with extra flour to cut the dough into 9 even slices. Place, cut-side up, on the prepared tray, allowing room for spreading. Cover loosely with plastic wrap. Set aside in a warm, draught-free place for 10-15 minutes or until doubled in size.

5 Preheat oven to 180°C. Bake for 25-30 minutes or until golden. Place tray on a wire rack. Set aside to cool.

6 To make the icing, place the icing sugar, milk and vanilla in a small heatproof bowl. Place the bowl over a small saucepan half-filled with simmering water (make sure the bowl doesn't touch the water). Stir for 1-2 minutes or until warm. Drizzle over the scrolls. Set aside for 10-15 minutes or until the icing is set.

○ GLUTEN FREE ○ MAKE AHEAD ○ FREEZABLE ● KID FRIENDLY ○ EASY

60 minutes prep

STEP-BY-STEP HOW TO GUIDE

Our Danish pastries are deliciously sweet and sticky. Use these tips to turn the dough into flaky pastry.

1 When making the dough, top with the butter, leaving a border so it won't come out the sides when rolling.

2 Fold short side furthest away from you over the centre. Fold short side closest to you over to enclose the butter.

3 Turn the dough 90 degrees. Pinch the edges together and roll. This incorporates the butter into the dough.

LEMON & RASPBERRY MAGIC CAKE

This should be in everyone's bag of baking tricks to wow friends and family. What comes out has a fudgy base, custard filling and sponge-cake top.

SERVES 12 **PREP** 20 mins **COOK** 1 hour

4 eggs, separated, at room temperature
210g (1⅓ cups) icing sugar mixture, plus extra, to dust
2 tsp finely grated lemon rind
2 tbs fresh lemon juice
100g (⅔ cup) plain flour
120g butter, melted, cooled
600ml milk, slightly warmed
1 tbs caster sugar
125g fresh raspberries, plus extra, to serve
Double cream, to serve

1 Preheat the oven to 180°C/160°C fan forced. Grease a square 21cm (base measurement) cake pan and line with baking paper, allowing the paper to overhang on two sides.

2 Use electric beaters to beat the egg yolks and icing sugar in a large bowl until very pale and thick. Beat in the lemon rind and juice until combined.

3 Beat in the flour until combined. Pour in the butter and beat until well combined. With the beaters on low speed, gradually add the milk and beat until well combined.

4 Use electric beaters with the whisk attachment to whisk the egg whites in a bowl until firm peaks form. Beat in caster sugar until well combined and the mixture holds firm peaks when the beaters are lifted.

5 Use a large spoon to fold one-third of the egg white into the flour mixture. Repeat in 2 more batches until just combined. Pour into the prepared pan and sprinkle with the raspberries.

6 Bake for 1 hour or until the cake is set but wobbles slightly. Set aside in the pan to cool completely. Carefully cut into slices and dust with extra icing sugar. Serve with double cream and extra raspberries.

COOK'S TIP

The cake can be made a day or two ahead. Store in the fridge in an airtight container. Remove from the fridge about 30 minutes before serving.

○ GLUTEN FREE ○ MAKE AHEAD ○ FREEZABLE ● KID FRIENDLY ● EASY

20
minutes
prep

★★★★★ *Definitely worth making. We rarely eat dessert, but this is easy to cook, light & not too sweet, just a small tasty treat to finish off our evening meal.* **PAUL WEBB**

STEP-BY-STEP
HOW-TO GUIDE

Follow our steps, pop the cake in the oven and wait for the magic to happen.

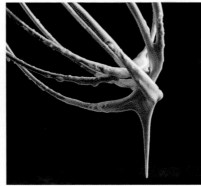

1 Lining your baking tin with the edges overhanging will help you to lift the cake out of the pan. It's important to use a square 21cm (base measurement) cake pan. If your pan is larger than this, the layers may not form evenly.

2 Beat the yolks and icing sugar until the mixture has turned pale yellow. Make sure the mixture is thick enough before adding the flour and remaining ingredients – a ribbon trail should form when the beaters are lifted.

3 With the motor running, slowly add the lemon zest and juice, then the flour, melted butter and milk. This cake uses more milk than a normal butter cake. The batter will be thin, almost like a crepe batter.

4 Chilled egg whites don't whip very well, so bring your eggs to room temperature before starting. Also make sure your mixer bowl and whisk are completely dry and clean, otherwise the mixture might not form peaks.

5 When adding the egg whites to the cake mixture, use a large dry metal spoon to very gently fold in the egg white. It's normal for the mixture to have a few lumpy bits, as this helps the batter separate into layers.

6 Pour the cake mixture into the prepared pan, then sprinkle with the raspberries. You don't need to press the raspberries in, as they will sink a little into the mixture as the cake cooks.

★★★★★

Turned out perfectly with beautiful flavour. Will be a favourite for sure. Leftover cake stayed fresh in the fridge for a couple of days.

FOXWOODS

MOCHA SELF-SAUCING PUDDING

The beauty of self-saucing puddings is they take very little time to prepare and you only need basic ingredients – perfect for indulging on a budget.

SERVES 6 **PREP** 15 mins (+ standing) **COOK** 40 mins

150g (1 cup) self-raising flour
4 tbs cocoa powder
100g (½ cup) caster sugar
125ml (½ cup) milk
1 egg
70g butter, melted
80g (½ cup, lightly packed)
   brown sugar
375ml (1½ cups) boiling water
1 tbs instant coffee granules or
   1 tbs coffee powder
Double cream, to serve

1 Preheat oven to 180°C/160°C fan forced. Brush a 1.5L (6 cup) ovenproof baking dish with melted butter. Place on a baking tray lined with baking paper.

2 Sift the flour and 2 tbs cocoa into a bowl. Stir in caster sugar. Whisk the milk, egg and butter in a jug until combined. Add to the flour mixture. Use a wooden spoon to stir until smooth. Pour into the prepared dish. Use the back of a spoon to smooth the surface.

3 Place the brown sugar in a bowl and sift the remaining 2 tbs cocoa over the sugar. Stir until well combined. Sprinkle the cocoa mixture evenly over the top of the pudding mixture.

4 Combine the boiling water and coffee in a jug. Gradually pour the coffee mixture over the back of a metal spoon onto the pudding.

5 Bake for 40 minutes or until a cake-like surface forms and a skewer inserted halfway into the centre comes out clean. Stand pudding for 5 minutes. Serve with cream.

COOK'S TIP

To increase the indulgence, stir 1 tbs Kahlua into the milk mixture before adding to the dry ingredients.

★★★★★ *All the family loved it, turned out beautifully.*
CMCNAMEE

○ GLUTEN FREE ○ MAKE AHEAD ○ FREEZABLE ○ KID FRIENDLY ● **EASY**

STEP-BY-STEP
HOW-TO GUIDE

Learn the secrets to the magic of self-saucing pudding – it's easy!

1 Sifting the self-raising flour and cocoa into a bowl before mixing with the other ingredients helps the mixture to rise and create the light cakey texture of the top layer of the pudding.

2 After pouring the pudding mixture into the greased dish, use the back of a large metal spoon to level the surface. This will help the finished pudding to have a smooth surface.

3 The brown sugar mixture and boiling water will sink to the bottom of the cake during cooking (adding a little moisture to the cake as it passes through), to create the sauce layer.

4 Slowly pouring the hot coffee mixture over the back of a metal spoon onto the pudding stops the liquid making holes in the sponge, so that the pudding rises evenly.

5 To test if the pudding is ready, only insert the skewer halfway – it should come out clean. If the skewer goes all the way in, you'll hit the sauce and you won't know if it's cooked.

6 Standing the pudding for 5 minutes after it's cooked allows the sauce to thicken slightly before serving. For best results, serve hot, otherwise the cake will soak up some of the sauce.

★★★★★ *There's something so comforting about puddings like this – great for a cosy winter treat.* **ADELE88**

CITRUS CREAM PASTRY HORNS

You only need five ingredients to make this shortcut version of the pastry classic, and it makes 20 horns, perfect for entertaining!

MAKES 20   **PREP** 25 mins (+ cooling)   **COOK** 1 hour

2 sheets butter puff pastry, just thawed
2 eggs, whisked
600ml thickened cream
160g (½ cup) lemon curd
55g (⅓ cup) pistachio kernels, finely chopped

1 Preheat oven to 200°C. Line 2 baking trays with baking paper. Cut pastry sheets into 2.5cm-wide strips. Spray five 9cm-long metal cream horn moulds with oil. Wrap the pastry, overlapping slightly, around the moulds. Brush with whisked egg. Bake for 12-15 minutes or until golden. Slide pastry off the moulds. Set aside to cool completely Repeat, in 4 batches, with remaining pastry.

2 Whisk cream until soft peaks form. Swirl in lemon curd. Place in a piping bag fitted with a 1.5cm round nozzle. Fill the horns with cream mixture and top with finely chopped pistachio kernels. Serve immediately.

COOK'S TIP

If you don't have a piping bag for the cream mixture, use a large sealable plastic bag with one corner cut off.

★★★★★ *Absolutely brilliant! So easy and impressive. I used ice-cream cones for the moulds and they worked fine.* **DEM14DEM**

○ GLUTEN FREE ○ MAKE AHEAD ○ FREEZABLE ● KID FRIENDLY ● EASY

STEP-BY-STEP HOW TO GUIDE

Filled with a sweet citrus cream, our flaky pastry horns are a top treat. Master them with these tips.

1 To prevent the pastry from sticking, spray metal cream horn moulds with olive oil spray.

2 If you don't have horn moulds, use mini ice-cream cones instead. Wrap them in a layer of foil.

3 Starting from the base, wrap the pastry strips, overlapping slightly, around the moulds or cones.

CHOC-MALLOW WHOOPIES

Bite into a chocolate sponge, then enjoy the burst of sweet marshmallow filling in these beautiful whoopie cakes.

MAKES 26 **PREP** 45 mins (+ cooling) **COOK** 30 mins

125g butter, at room temperature
160g (1 cup, lightly packed) brown sugar
1 tsp vanilla extract
1 egg
50g (½ cup) cocoa powder, sifted
1 tsp bicarbonate of soda
300g (2 cups) plain flour
330ml (1⅓ cups) buttermilk

MARSHMALLOW FILLING
3 egg whites
270g (1¼ cups) caster sugar
2 tbs glucose syrup
1 tsp vanilla extract
Pinch of salt

1 Preheat oven to 190°C/170°C fan-forced. Line 2 baking trays with baking paper. Place the butter, sugar and vanilla in a bowl and use electric beaters to beat until pale and creamy. Beat in the egg.

2 Stir in the cocoa and bicarb. Fold in the flour and buttermilk, in alternating batches, until just smooth. The mixture should be a little stiff.

3 Use a 3cm-diameter ice-cream scoop to place rounds of the mixture onto prepared trays, leaving room for spreading. Use your finger to smooth mixture around the edges.

4 Bake, swapping the trays halfway through cooking, for 10 minutes or until firm. Cool slightly on the trays. Place on a wire rack to cool completely. Repeat, in 2 more batches, with the remaining mixture.

5 To make the marshmallow filling, whisk the egg whites, sugar, glucose, vanilla and salt in a heatproof bowl over a pan of simmering water for 10 minutes or until a ribbon trail forms when the whisk is lifted.

6 Transfer the marshmallow mixture to a clean bowl. Use electric beaters to beat for 5-8 minutes or until the mixture is cooled, thick and holds its shape.

7 Place half the whoopies, base-side up, on a clean work surface. Spoon the marshmallow filling into a piping bag fitted with a 1cm fluted nozzle. Pipe filling onto half the whoopies, leaving a 2mm border. Top with the remaining whoopies and press lightly to sandwich together. Serve.

★★★★★ *These were great fun to make with my daughter for her office bake sale and lovely flavour. Using the ice-cream scoop really helped make them perfect.* **PIEMAKERPARTY**

○ GLUTEN FREE ○ MAKE AHEAD ○ FREEZABLE ● KID FRIENDLY ○ EASY

STEP-BY-STEP
HOW-TO GUIDE

How to make these pies look perfect? Let us show you all the tricks!

1 Beat the butter, sugar and vanilla until pale yellow and you can't feel the grains of sugar. Make sure you use butter that's at room temperature – this helps aerate the mixture.

2 Use a large metal spoon to gently fold the flour and buttermilk into the butter mixture until just smooth – be careful not to overmix. The mixture should be a little stiff.

3 If you don't have an ice-cream scoop, use a tablespoon. Dip the scoop or spoon into hot water, then dry, about every 10 scoops to easily get the mixture off the scoop.

4 When making the filling, don't let the bowl touch the simmering water and whisk constantly. 'Ribbon stage' means that when you lift the whisk, the mixture falls and forms a ribbon that will hold its shape.

5 Transferring the marshmallow mixture to a second bowl to continue mixing is important because you want it to cool down and thicken into a consistency that is suitable for piping.

6 If you don't have a piping bag fitted with a nozzle, you can use two teaspoons to dollop the marshmallow filling on the whoopie bases instead. Place the whoopies in the fridge until ready to serve.

CHOCOLATE & PEANUT BUTTER WHOOPIES: Make chocolate whoopies, omitting marshmallow filling. Use electric beaters to beat 125g cream cheese, at room temperature, and 70g (¼ cup) smooth peanut butter in a bowl. Beat in 230g (1½ cups) icing sugar mixture. Add ½ teaspoon milk. Beat until pale and creamy. Spoon peanut butter frosting into a piping bag fitted with a 5mm fluted nozzle. Pipe half the whoopies with frosting. Sandwich with remaining whoopies. Drizzle over 100g melted dark chocolate.

CHOC-MINT WHOOPIES: Melt 200g Lindt Excellence Mint Intense and 160ml (⅔ cup) thickened cream in a microwave-safe bowl on High, stirring every minute, until smooth. Add 100g chopped butter. Stir until smooth. Place in fridge for 1-1½ hours or until thick. Beat with electric beaters until pale and creamy. Make chocolate whoopies, omitting marshmallow filling. Spoon choc mint ganache into a piping bag fitted with a 1cm fluted nozzle. Pipe half the whoopies with ganache. Sandwich with remaining whoopies. Spread tops with 200g melted dark chocolate. Top with chopped Nestlé Peppermint Crisp.

COCONUT & LEMON CURD WHOOPIES: For the whoopies, replace vanilla with coconut essence. Replace cocoa powder with 45g (½ cup) desiccated coconut. Reduce the buttermilk to 250ml (1 cup). For the lemon glacé icing, whisk 1 egg white in a large bowl until frothy. Gradually whisk in 250g sifted pure icing sugar until smooth and glossy. Whisk in 1½ teaspoons lemon juice and 3 drops lemon food colouring. For the filling, whisk 250g mascarpone and 95g (⅓ cup) lemon curd in a bowl until mixture thickens and just holds its shape. Spoon filling into a piping bag fitted with a 1cm round nozzle. Pipe half the whoopies with filling. Sandwich with remaining whoopies. Spread tops with icing and top with roasted coconut chips.

RASPBERRIES & CREAM CHOC CAKES

Raspberries and chocolate are an ideal match in these dreamy patisserie-worthy treats, ready for any occasion needing extra-special flair.

MAKES 4 **PREP** 1 hour (+ cooling) **COOK** 20 mins

60g butter, at room temperature
55g (¼ cup, firmly packed)
  brown sugar
1 tsp vanilla bean paste
100g milk chocolate, melted, cooled
1 egg
75g (½ cup) self-raising flour
80ml (⅓ cup) buttermilk
300ml ctn double cream
125g fresh raspberries, plus extra,
  to decorate
1 tbs raspberry jam
Icing sugar, to dust

1 Preheat oven to 180°C. Line a baking tray with baking paper. Stack two 7.5cm egg rings on prepared tray. Repeat with 6 more rings to make 4 stacks. Cut four 7.5 x 32cm strips of baking paper. Spray with oil. Line stacks with the strips.

2 Use electric beaters to beat the butter, sugar and vanilla in a bowl until pale and creamy. Beat in the chocolate until smooth. Add the egg. Beat until combined. Fold in the flour alternately with buttermilk. Spoon among stacks and smooth surfaces. Bake for 20 minutes or until a skewer inserted into centres comes out clean. Set aside on the tray on a wire rack to cool completely.

3 Remove egg rings. Cut each cake horizontally into 3 layers. Whisk the cream in a bowl until soft peaks form. Mash raspberries and jam in a bowl.

4 Divide the cake bases, cut-side up, among serving plates. Top with a dollop of cream and a spoonful of the raspberry mixture. Continue layering with remaining cake, cream and raspberry mixture, finishing with cake. Decorate with extra raspberries and dust with icing sugar.

COOK'S TIP

You can make the cakes up to 1 day ahead. Store in an airtight container, then fill with cream and decorate just before serving.

★★★★★ *I made these for a special bridal high tea and they were perfect, just like the picture.* **LEMONLIME19**

○ GLUTEN FREE ● MAKE AHEAD ○ FREEZABLE ● KID FRIENDLY ○ EASY

STEP-BY-STEP HOW TO GUIDE

For perfectly shaped individual cakes, you need to get the preparation spot-on.

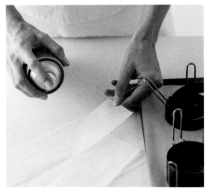

1 To stop cakes from sticking and to make it easier to remove from the stacked egg rings, spray paper with oil.

2 To support the cakes as they rise, allow the baking paper strips to extend above the stacked egg rings.

3 For level cake layers, smooth the surface of the batter so the cakes rise evenly within the egg rings.

CHOC-ORANGE RICOTTA TART

For an amazing slice to go with coffee, encase a bittersweet dark chocolate filling with hints of orange and spices in a nutty almond pastry.

SERVES 10 **PREP** 40 mins (+ cooling, chilling & resting) **COOK** 1 hour

60g (⅓ cup) blanched almonds, toasted
40g (¼ cup) sesame seeds, toasted
190g (1¼ cups) plain flour
125g butter, chilled, chopped
55g (¼ cup) caster sugar
2 eggs
½ tsp vanilla extract
Melted butter, to grease
1 tbs demerara sugar

RICOTTA FILLING
500g fresh ricotta
100g (½ cup) caster sugar
2 eggs
100g dark chocolate (70% cocoa), finely chopped
2 tsp finely grated orange rind
2 tbs pine nuts, toasted, chopped
½ tsp ground cinnamon

1 Process the almonds and sesame seeds in a food processor until finely chopped. Add the flour, butter and caster sugar and process until the mixture resembles fine breadcrumbs. Add 1 egg and the vanilla. Process until dough just starts to come together.

2 Turn dough onto a floured surface. Knead lightly until just smooth. Shape into a disc. Cover with plastic wrap. Place in fridge for 4-6 hours to rest.

3 Meanwhile, to make the ricotta filling, use electric beaters to beat the ricotta and sugar in a bowl until smooth. Add the eggs, 1 at a time, beating well after each addition. Stir in the chocolate, orange rind, pine nuts and cinnamon.

4 Lightly brush a 3cm-deep, 24cm (base measurement) fluted tart tin with removable base with the melted butter. Roll pastry between 2 sheets of non-stick baking paper until 4mm thick. Line tin with the pastry. Trim. Reserve excess pastry. Cover tin and excess pastry with plastic wrap. Place in the fridge for 30 minutes to rest.

5 Preheat oven to 180°C. Fill pastry case with the ricotta filling. Smooth the surface. Whisk the remaining egg in a bowl. Brush pastry edge with the egg.

6 Roll the reserved pastry into a 26 x 20cm rectangle. Cut lengthways into twelve 1.5cm-wide strips. Arrange strips in a lattice pattern over the filling. Press the edges to seal. Trim excess. Brush with egg and sprinkle with the demerara sugar. Bake for 45 minutes to 1 hour or until golden and filling has set. Set aside to cool slightly. Place in fridge to chill. Remove 1 hour before serving.

COOK'S TIP

If your pastry is too firm to roll out, stand at room temperature for 10-15 minutes before proceeding.

○ GLUTEN FREE ● MAKE AHEAD ○ FREEZABLE ○ KID FRIENDLY ○ EASY

STEP-BY-STEP HOW TO GUIDE

Here's how to prepare the pastry for this beautiful Italian-style lattice tart.

1 To give the tart shell a neat finish, line the tin with pastry and press into the fluted side. Trim excess.

2 To make the lattice, roll out the reserved pastry and cut into 12 strips, 1.5cm wide and 26cm long.

3 Arrange 6 strips evenly in each direction on top of the tart, using the scraps to patch up any tears.

CHAI-SPICED CUSTARD TARTS

With puff pastry and creamy custard, these super-easy sweet bites are perfect for afternoon tea, bake sales and more.

MAKES 18 **PREP** 40 mins (+ infusing, chilling & cooling) **COOK** 35 mins

Melted butter, to grease
150ml pouring cream
125ml (½ cup) milk
100g (½ cup) caster sugar
8 cardamom pods, lightly crushed
6 black peppercorns
1 black tea bag
1 cinnamon stick
½ tsp ground ginger
Little pinch ground nutmeg
6 egg yolks
3 sheets frozen puff pastry, thawed
Plain flour, to dust
40g (¼ cup) pistachios, finely chopped
Icing sugar, to dust

1 Use a pastry brush to lightly grease eighteen 80ml (⅓ cup) muffin pans with melted butter. Place the greased pans in the fridge to chill, while preparing the custard filling.

2 Place the cream, milk, sugar, cardamom, peppercorns, tea, cinnamon, ginger and nutmeg in a saucepan over medium heat. Bring to the boil. Remove immediately from the heat. Set aside for 2 hours to infuse.

3 Preheat oven to 180°C/160°C fan forced. Pour cream mixture through a fine sieve into a jug. Place yolks in a large bowl and, whisking constantly, gradually add cream mixture. Sieve mixture again and set aside.

4 Cut a pastry sheet in half and stack one half on top of the other. Roll up the pastry to form a tight log. Cut the log into 6 even portions. Repeat with the remaining pastry.

5 Roll out portions on a floured surface to 3mm-thick discs. Press into prepared pans. Trim excess. Place in the fridge for 15 minutes. Line with baking paper. Fill with ceramic pie weights or uncooked rice. Bake for 10 minutes. Remove paper and weights or rice.

6 Reduce oven to 160°C/140°C fan forced. Divide cream mixture among pastry. Bake for 20 minutes, until golden and custard is just set (mixture will wobble slightly). Sprinkle with pistachio. Set aside to cool. Dust with icing sugar.

COOK'S TIP

These tarts are best served at room temperature on the day of baking.

★★★★★ *I'm a big chai fan so these are right up my alley – love the flavours and perfect with a cuppa!* **BLUEICECREAM**

○ GLUTEN FREE ○ MAKE AHEAD ○ FREEZABLE ○ KID FRIENDLY ● EASY

40
minutes
prep

STEP-BY-STEP HOW TO GUIDE
Learn all the sneaky tricks for these perfectly golden delights.

1 After greasing the pan, place it in the fridge to chill. This will help the pastry to puff up during baking.

2 This method of preparing and rolling out the pastry is super-easy and adds extra flaky layers.

3 Divide the custard evenly among the pastry shells, so they're almost – but not completely – full.

PROFITEROLES WITH CHOCOLATE

Transform light-as-air pastry into glorious profiteroles filled with rich custard and finished with a glossy chocolate sauce.

MAKES 18   **PREP** 40 mins (+ cooling)   **COOK** 45 mins

80g butter, chopped, at room temperature
150g (1 cup) plain flour, sifted
3 eggs, at room temperature, whisked

CRÈME PÂTISSIÈRE
435ml (1¾ cups) milk
1 vanilla bean, split lengthways, seeds scraped
3 egg yolks
70g (⅓ cup) caster sugar
50g (⅓ cup) plain flour, sifted

CHOCOLATE SAUCE
200g dark chocolate, finely chopped
250ml (1 cup) thickened cream
1 tbs brown sugar

1 Place the butter and 250ml (1 cup) water in a saucepan. Bring just to the boil. Remove from the heat. Beat in flour. Return pan to medium heat and cook, stirring constantly, for 2-3 minutes or until mixture comes away from side of pan in a ball. Set aside to cool for 5 minutes.

2 Gradually add the egg, 1 tbs at a time, beating well after each addition until dough is thick and glossy.

3 Preheat oven to 200°C/180°C fan forced. Line 2 baking trays with baking paper. Place heaped dessertspoonfuls of dough, 3cm apart, on trays. Use wet hands to pat down any peaks. Sprinkle trays with water to create steam. Bake for 30-35 minutes or until puffed and golden.

4 Turn off the oven. Use the tip of a small sharp knife to pierce the base of each profiterole. Return profiteroles to the tray and place in the oven for 20 minutes to dry out. Transfer to a wire rack to cool.

5 Meanwhile, for crème pâtissière, heat milk and vanilla seeds in a saucepan over low heat. Whisk egg yolks and sugar in a bowl until thick. Whisk in flour, then milk mixture. Return to pan. Whisk over low heat for 5 minutes or until thickened. Transfer to a bowl and cover surface with plastic wrap. Chill in the fridge.

6 Spoon crème into a piping bag with a 5mm plain nozzle. Push nozzle into base of each profiterole and fill with crème.

7 For chocolate sauce, place chocolate, cream and sugar in a saucepan over low heat. Use a metal spoon to stir for 5 minutes or until smooth. Pour over profiteroles. Serve.

COOK'S TIP

You can make the pastry puffs to the end of Step 4 up to 1 week ahead. Store in an airtight container. To serve, place on a baking tray and heat in oven at 200°C for 10 minutes. Cool on a wire rack. Fill with crème pâtissière.

○ GLUTEN FREE   ● MAKE AHEAD   ○ FREEZABLE   ● KID FRIENDLY   ○ EASY

40 minutes prep

★★★★★ Great recipe. It worked a treat. Pastry puffed up well. **KERRYK18**

99

HOW-TO GUIDE

This restaurant classic is a must-make to impress at gatherings!

1 Have everything measured and ready before making the choux pastry for your profiteroles, so you can pay full attention to the cooking process. Chop the butter into small even pieces so it melts quickly and evenly.

2 Allow the mixture to cool for the full 5 minutes so the eggs don't cook when they are added in. Make sure the eggs are at room temperature – this will help the dough to rise and have a lovely puffy texture.

3 Make sure to leave enough room between the profiteroles so they have space to rise. Gently pat down any peaks with wet hands – this will help your profiteroles bake as perfect neat little balls.

4 Cutting a slit in the eclairs then returning them to the oven dries out the inside, so they won't be soggy when you fill them. Make sure the outside is crispy before you cut them, otherwise they may collapse.

5 Crème pâtissière means 'pastry cream' and is a custard that is thickened with flour, making it perfect for filling profiteroles. Cover the surface with plastic wrap to prevent a skin forming and allow to cool completely.

6 When filling the profiteroles, use the hole made in the profiteroles during baking. Tilt the nozzle of the piping bag gently each way to evenly fill with crème pâtissière. Drizzle with chocolate sauce just before serving.

★★★★★ *Best recipe I've found for profiteroles. Only problem is when we have a get together I am always having to make them.* RINNYJ

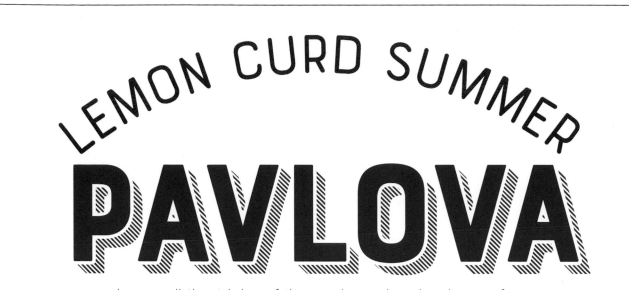

LEMON CURD SUMMER PAVLOVA

Learn all the tricks of the trade and make the perfect pavlova with a zingy summer citrus swirl.

SERVES 6 **PREP** 30 mins (+ cooling) **COOK** 1 hour 30 mins

6 egg whites
315g (1½ cups) caster sugar
1 tsp gluten-free cornflour
100ml thickened cream, whipped
    to firm peaks
1 mango, peeled, thinly sliced
4 lychees, peeled, halved, deseeded
1 banana, peeled, sliced diagonally
2 passionfruit, halved
20g (¼ cup) shredded coconut,
    lightly toasted

LEMON CURD

3 eggs
170g (¾ cup) caster sugar
2 tsp cornflour
2 lemons, juiced
2 limes, rind finely grated, juiced
20g butter, chopped

1 Preheat the oven to 140°C/120°C fan forced. Use electric beaters to beat the egg whites in a clean, dry bowl until soft peaks form.

2 Add the sugar, 1 tbs at a time, beating until dissolved and mixture is thick and glossy. Beat in cornflour.

3 Draw a 22cm circle on a sheet of baking paper. Place the paper, ink-side down, on a baking tray. Spoon the meringue onto the circle. Smooth around the edge of the meringue. Use a spatula to create swirls and peaks on top. Bake for 1 hour 30 minutes or until crisp and dry. Turn oven off. Leave meringue in oven, with door ajar, to cool completely.

4 Meanwhile, for the lemon curd, whisk the eggs, sugar and cornflour in a saucepan. Add lemon and lime juice and lime rind. Cook over medium heat, whisking, for 5-8 minutes, until thickened. Stir in the butter. Set aside to cool to room temperature. Transfer to a bowl, cover with plastic wrap and place in the fridge for 2-3 hours to chill.

5 Gently fold the whipped cream and lemon curd together in a bowl to create a marbled effect. Spoon over the meringue. Top with the mango, lychee and banana. Drizzle with passionfruit. Sprinkle with coconut.

COOK'S TIP

You can top this pavlova with any fruit you prefer – mixed berries also work well.

● GLUTEN FREE ○ MAKE AHEAD ○ FREEZABLE ● KID FRIENDLY ○ EASY

30 minutes prep

★★★★★ *This is a great pav and curd recipe.*
I make this curd often for other uses. It is fail safe! **KYLES1**

STEP-BY-STEP
HOW-TO GUIDE

Make a show-stopper meringue with these easy steps.

1 Chilled egg whites don't whip very well, so bring your eggs to room temperature before starting. The egg whites reach soft peaks when they cling to the beaters but are still a little foamy.

2 Keep the motor running on the mixer while you slowly and steadily add the sugar. If the mixture is grainy when rubbed between your fingers, continue beating.

3 Use a little meringue on each corner of the baking paper to act as a glue when you line the baking tray, so it stays in place while you're shaping the meringue.

4 An offset palette knife or spatula is the best tool to spread and shape the meringue. Roughing up the sides creates a little crater in the meringue, perfect for holding the toppings.

5 Keep whisking the lemon curd as it cooks to keep the texture even, making sure it thickens withpout becoming lumpy. Cut the butter into small pieces so it incorporates evenly.

6 Use a large metal spoon to gently fold the chilled lemon curd into the whisked cream, to create a rippled effect, keeping as much airiness in the cream as possible.

★★★★★ *This is such a great pav — the meringue has a great marshmallow texture on the inside and the tropical fruit has that lovely sweetness and tang.* **STRAWBERRYPIE**

MOLTEN CHOCOLATE, SOUFFLE

With its airy texture, oozy truffle centre and wicked dark chocolate flavour, this easy sweet soufflé recipe is everything you want it to be.

SERVES 4 **PREP** 20 mins (+ cooling) **COOK** 40 mins

200g dark chocolate, finely chopped
100g butter, chopped
100g (½ cup) caster sugar
50g (⅓ cup) plain flour
4 eggs, separated
Pinch of cream of tartar
2 tbs caster sugar, extra
8 Lindt Lindor Dark Chocolate Balls
Double cream, to serve

SAUCE
100g dark chocolate, finely chopped
60ml (¼ cup) thickened cream
10g butter

1 Preheat oven to 180°C and grease four 310ml (1¼-cup-capacity) ovenproof dishes with butter.

2 Melt chocolate and butter in a large glass or ceramic bowl in the microwave on High, stirring every minute until smooth. Cool for 5 minutes.

3 Stir the sugar, flour and egg yolks into the chocolate mixture until well combined.

4 Use electric beaters to whisk the egg whites and cream of tartar in a large bowl until soft peaks form. Add extra sugar and whisk until firm peaks form. Use a large metal spoon to fold into the chocolate mixture until combined.

5 Divide chocolate mixture among the greased dishes. Press 2 chocolate balls into the centre of the chocolate mixture in each dish. Bake for 30-35 minutes until well risen.

6 For the sauce, heat the chocolate, cream and butter in a heatproof jug in the microwave on High, stirring every minute until melted and smooth. Serve puddings with sauce and double cream.

COOK'S TIP

You can use any ovenproof dishes or pots you like for this recipe, bit it's best for the dishes to have straight sides, which will help the soufflés rise properly.

★★★★★ *I was so happy with how these turned out, I made them again the next weekend!* **RONSAUSAGE**

○ GLUTEN FREE ○ MAKE AHEAD ○ FREEZABLE ○ KID FRIENDLY ● **EASY**

STEP-BY-STEP HOW TO GUIDE

Here's how to create a light yet rich chocolate soufflé that will wow the crowd.

1 For smooth chocolate, stir with a dry metal – not wooden – spoon, to ensure no moisture gets into the mixture.

2 To add volume without overbeating, whisk the sugar into the eggwhites at soft peak stage.

3 For molten centres, completely cover the Lindt chocolate balls with the mixture.

STICKY DATE PUDDING WITH BUTTERSCOTCH

The dates in this sticky pudding help to keep it moist, while the fresh ginger and ground spices add a subtle warmth.

SERVES 12 **PREP** 20 mins (+ cooling) **COOK** 1 hour 10 mins

400g fresh dates, pitted,
    coarsely chopped
375ml (1½ cups) boiling water
1 tsp bicarbonate of soda
1 tsp grated fresh ginger
100g butter, at room temperature
215g (1 cup) caster sugar
3 eggs
225g (1½ cups) self-raising flour
½ tsp mixed spice
¼ tsp ground cloves
Double cream, to serve

BUTTERSCOTCH SAUCE
200g (1 cup, firmly packed)
    brown sugar
250ml (1 cup) thickened cream
60g butter
2 tbs golden syrup

1 Preheat the oven to 180°C/160°C fan forced. Grease a round 22cm (base measurement) cake pan with melted butter. Line the base of the pan with baking paper.

2 Place the dates and water in a medium saucepan over high heat. Bring to the boil. Stir in the bicarb. Set aside for 10 minutes to cool slightly. Stir in the ginger.

3 Using electric beaters, beat the butter and sugar in a bowl until pale and creamy. Add the eggs, 1 at a time, beating well after each addition. Stir in the date mixture, flour, mixed spice and cloves until well combined.

4 Pour mixture into the prepared pan. Bake for 1 hour or until a skewer inserted into the centre of the cake comes out clean. Use a skewer to pierce holes in the hot cake.

5 For the sauce, stir sugar, cream, butter and golden syrup in a medium saucepan over medium heat for 3-4 minutes or until smooth. Bring to the boil. Reduce heat to medium-low. Simmer for 1-2 minutes or until thickened.

6 Pour 125ml (½ cup) sauce over the cake. Set aside for 10 minutes. Run a butter knife around the pan and remove the cake. Serve with cream and remaining sauce.

COOK'S TIP

You can use a store-bought butterscotch or caramel sauce, if you like – just heat and serve on the side.

○ GLUTEN FREE   ○ MAKE AHEAD   ○ FREEZABLE   ● KID FRIENDLY   ● EASY

★★★★★ *Absolutely lovely cake. Everyone enjoyed it. Very moist and the sauce is beautiful with it.* **STARMIE**

STEP-BY-STEP
HOW-TO GUIDE

This family favourite is simple to make – and a must-make dessert!

1 Greasing the base of the pan helps to hold the baking paper in place without any creases that could make an indent in the cake. Greasing the sides will make the cake easy to remove.

2 The dates add a natural toffee flavour to the pudding. We used fresh dates, such as medjool. They are available from the fresh produce section of the supermarket.

3 Adding the eggs one at a time helps them to incorporate properly into the mixture. Next, use a large spoon to stir in the date mixture and dry ingredients.

4 You can use the same thin skewer you used to test if the cake is cooked to pierce holes in the hot cake. The holes make it easier for the cake to absorb the hot butterscotch syrup.

5 You can make the butterscotch sauce ahead of time and store in an airtight jar in the fridge for up to 2 days. Return to the heat and bring to a simmer before pouring over the cake.

6 After pouring some of the sauce over the cake, set cake aside for the full 10 minutes so the sauce has time to absorb. This is what gives the cake the moist, pudding-like texture.

★★★★★ This is a gorgeous recipe, serves many and my (big) kids love it! Every time I visit its the first thing I cook! **WEBSTERDM5**

WOW DESSERTS

SPATULAS AT THE READY! THESE CRAZY GOOD OVER-THE-TOP BAKES ARE GUARANTEED TO IMPRESS. GLAMOROUS LAYER CAKES, JAW-DROPPING PAVS AND STUNNING SLICES ALL AWAIT.

SALTED CARAMEL PRETZEL CAKE

Reach for the sky with our pretzel-lined chocolate cake, crowned with gloriously bronzed meringue and drizzles of caramel.

SERVES 16 **PREP** 1 hour (+ cooling & chilling) **COOK** 2 hours

125ml (½ cup) salted caramel topping, plus extra, to decorate
110g pretzels
180g dark chocolate (70% cocoa), finely chopped
10 thick pretzel sticks

CHOCOLATE MUD CAKES
500g unsalted butter, chopped
360g dark chocolate, coarsely chopped
4 eggs
530g (2½ cups) caster sugar
200g (1⅓ cups) plain flour
100g (⅔ cup) self-raising flour
95g (1 cup) cocoa powder
½ tsp bicarbonate of soda
235g (1 cup) sour cream
125ml (½ cup) milk

SWISS MERINGUE BUTTERCREAM
4 egg whites
215g (1 cup) caster sugar
400g unsalted butter, chopped, at room temperature
180g milk chocolate, melted, cooled
180g dark chocolate (70% cocoa), melted, cooled

ITALIAN MERINGUE
215g (1 cup) caster sugar
3 egg whites
Pinch of cream of tartar

1 Preheat oven to 180°C/160°C fan forced. Grease the base and side of 2 round 20cm (base measurement) cake pans and line with baking paper.

2 For the cakes, heat butter and chocolate in a saucepan over low heat, stirring constantly, for 2-4 minutes until melted and smooth. Stand for 10 minutes.

3 Use a balloon whisk to whisk the eggs into the chocolate mixture, 1 at a time. Whisk in the sugar, flours, cocoa and bicarb. Whisk in the sour cream and milk until combined. Divide evenly between prepared pans. Bake for 1½ hours or until a skewer inserted in centre of each cake comes out clean. Transfer to a wire rack. Set aside in the pans to cool completely.

4 For the meringue buttercream, whisk egg whites and sugar in a heatproof bowl. Place bowl over a saucepan of simmering water (don't let the water touch the bowl). Use a balloon whisk to stir for 10-15 minutes or until the sugar dissolves and mixture reaches 70°C on a cook's thermometer. Transfer mixture to a clean bowl. Use electric beaters to beat for 5 minutes or until firm peaks form and mixture is almost at room temperature. Add the butter, a few pieces at a time, beating well after each addition until mixture is thick and smooth.

5 Place half the buttercream in a separate bowl. Add milk chocolate to 1 bowl and beat until combined. Place in fridge for 5 minutes.

6 Use a large, sharp knife to trim the tops of the cakes to flatten them, if needed. Cut both cakes in half horizontally. Place 1 cake layer on a serving plate. Spread the top with a third of the milk chocolate buttercream. Drizzle with 2 tbs caramel topping. Top with 1 more cake layer and half the remaining milk chocolate buttercream. Drizzle with another 2 tbs caramel topping. Repeat with the remaining cakes, milk chocolate buttercream and caramel topping, finishing with a cake layer. Place in the fridge for 30 minutes to chill.

7 Add dark chocolate to the remaining buttercream. Beat until combined. Place in the fridge for 5 minutes. Use a palette knife to spread over the top and side of the cake. Decorate the side of the cake with pretzels. Place in the fridge for 1 hour to chill.

8 Meanwhile, line a tray with baking paper. Place the chocolate in a microwave-safe bowl. Cook on Medium, stirring every 30 seconds, for 5 minutes or until melted. Dip pretzel sticks in chocolate to coat 1 end. Place

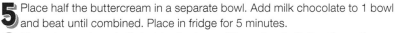

○ GLUTEN FREE ○ MAKE AHEAD ○ FREEZABLE ● KID FRIENDLY ○ EASY

on prepared tray. Transfer to the fridge for 5 minutes to set. Reserve any leftover chocolate.

9 For Italian meringue, stir sugar and 60ml (¼ cup) water in a saucepan over low heat until sugar dissolves, brushing side of pan with a wet pastry brush. Cook over medium-high heat, without stirring, for 3-5 minutes or until syrup reaches 115°C (soft ball stage) on a cook's thermometer. While syrup continues to cook, use an electric stand mixer with a whisk attachment to whisk the egg whites and cream of tartar until soft peaks form. When syrup reaches 121°C (hard ball stage), slowly add it to the egg white mixture. Whisk on high speed until mixture is thick.

10 Spoon meringue onto cake, making swirls. Top with pretzel sticks. Use a kitchen blowtorch to caramelise meringue. Reheat reserved chocolate until just runny. Drizzle over cake with extra caramel topping.

STEP-BY-STEP
HOW-TO GUIDE

For a towering layer cake that is absolute perfection, check out our top tips.

1 When whisking the egg whites and sugar over the simmering water, don't leave it too late to use the thermometer to check the temperature or the egg may overcook.

2 Make sure the chocolate has cooled to room temperature before adding it to the buttercream. If it's too hot, it will start to melt the buttercream, making it too soft to work with.

3 Use a large sharp knife to slice the cakes in half horizontally. To help keep your layers even, insert toothpicks around the side of the cake at the same height, and cut just above them.

4 An offset palette knife is ideal to spread the buttercream over each cake layer, as it keeps your hands clear of the buttercream as you work. If you don't have a palette knife, a flat-bladed butter knife is the next best thing.

5 Attach pretzels to the cake straight after spreading the buttercream over. If you chill the cake first, the buttercream will set firm and pretzels won't stick. When attaching, gently press the pretzels into the buttercream.

6 When dipping pretzel sticks in the melted chocolate, allow any excess to drip into the bowl before transferring to the lined tray. To set the chocolate, put the tray in the fridge until you're ready to caramelise the meringue.

★★★★★ My birthday cake!!! SUMMER127

PASSIONA CURD PAVLOVA

Watch jaws drop when this golden wreath adorned with meringue kisses and filled with Passiona curd arrives on the table.

SERVES 10 **PREP** 1 hour (+ cooling) **COOK** 2 hours 35 mins

8 egg whites
430g (2 cups) caster sugar
2 tsp gluten-free cornflour
1 tsp white vinegar
1 tsp vanilla extract
Lemon yellow, orange and leaf green food pastes, to tint
200ml double cream
250ml (1 cup) thickened cream
2 passionfruits, pulp only

PASSIONA CURD
1 egg
55g (¼ cup) caster sugar
60g butter, chopped
80ml (⅓ cup) Passiona (sparkling passionfruit-flavoured drink)
2 passionfruits, pulp only

1 Preheat oven to 120°C/100°C fan forced. Draw a 21cm circle on a sheet of baking paper. Place the baking paper, ink-side down, on a baking tray.

2 Use electric beaters to whisk 4 egg whites in a clean, dry bowl until firm peaks form. Add 215g (1 cup) caster sugar, 1 tbs at a time, beating constantly, until sugar dissolves and mixture is thick and glossy. Beat in the cornflour, vinegar and vanilla until just combined. Spoon mixture onto baking paper, using circle as a guide. Smooth top and side. Bake for 1 hour 30 minutes or until meringue is crisp and dry. Turn off oven. Cool meringue in oven, with door closed.

3 Prepare 3 piping bags: one fitted with a 1cm plain nozzle, one with a 1cm star nozzle and one with a 1cm open star nozzle. Place them upright in tall glasses. Combine ½ tsp yellow dye with a few drops of orange dye in a small bowl to make a passionfruit colour. In a separate bowl, combine ½ tsp yellow dye with a few drops of green dye to make green-yellow.

4 Reheat oven to 120°C/100°C fan forced. Draw a 22cm circle on a sheet of baking paper. Draw an 11cm circle inside the large circle. Place paper, ink-side down, on a baking tray. Using electric beaters, whisk remaining egg whites in a clean, dry bowl until firm peaks form. Add remaining 215g (1 cup) caster sugar, 1 tbs at a time, beating constantly, until sugar dissolves and mixture is thick and glossy.

5 Lightly paint 3 long stripes of passionfruit colour into the plain nozzle bag. Paint 4 stripes of green-yellow into the open star nozzle bag. Spoon meringue into each piping bag. Use circles as a guide to randomly pipe plain meringue, in different sizes, onto the paper. Repeat with remaining meringue to form a wreath. Bake for 1 hour to 1 hour 30 minutes until meringue is crisp and dry. Turn off oven. Cool meringue in oven, with door closed.

6 For the curd, whisk egg, sugar, butter, Passiona and passionfruit pulp in a large microwave-safe bowl until combined. Microwave on High, stirring every 30 seconds, for 3-5 minutes, until a smooth, thick curd forms. Cool completely.

7 Beat creams to firm peaks. Top meringue base with a thin layer of cream. Spoon some curd onto the centre. Spoon cream around the side. Drizzle with passionfruit pulp. Top with the wreath. Serve with remaining cream and curd.

● GLUTEN FREE ● MAKE AHEAD ○ FREEZABLE ● KID FRIENDLY ○ EASY

★★★★★ *Made it as a birthday cake for a Passiona-loving friend. Gorgeous colours.* **GARDENINGGAL**

60 minutes prep

STEP-BY-STEP
HOW-TO GUIDE

Here's how to make the mini meringue wreath for this delightful pavlova.

1 Start with the white meringue and pipe as much white as you can to have a good coating on the base of the plain meringue.

2 Repeat with the passionfruit meringue, making large and small piping and swirls. Leave gaps for the green-yellow meringue.

3 Repeat with the green-yellow meringue, making large and small piping and swirls. These will turn golden after baking.

4 Finish with the remaining white meringue, filling in any gaps on the wreath. Add a few more coloured swirls on top, too, if needed.

5 Spread a thin layer of cream over the meringue base, then dollop some more around its outer edge. Pour a little Passiona curd in the middle.

6 Top the curd with a thin layer of cream. Decorate with extra fresh passionfruit pulp. Top with the mini meringue wreath.

★★★★★ *This takes pav to a whole new level! Love it as an alternative Christmas wreath.* **EFFIEBEANS**

GOLDEN GAYTIME SLICE

Thought your favourite Aussie toffee ice-cream couldn't get any better? Think again! This sweet slice is a bona fide game changer.

MAKES 9 **PREP** 30 mins (+ cooling & freezing) **COOK** 1 hour 30 mins

200g white chocolate, finely chopped
125g unsalted butter
3 eggs
300g (2 cups) plain flour
100g (½ cup) caster sugar
70g (⅓ cup, firmly packed) brown sugar
2 tbs golden syrup
400g milk chocolate, finely chopped
60ml (¼ cup) vegetable oil
125g malt biscuits, coarsely crushed
2 x 400ml pkt Golden Gaytime 4-pack ice-creams
Caramel spread or sauce, to serve

CHOCOLATE BASE
75g (½ cup) plain flour
40g (¼ cup) self-raising flour
55g (¼ cup, firmly packed) brown sugar
1 tbs cocoa powder
90g butter, melted

1 Preheat oven to 180°C/160°C fan forced. Line an 18cm (base measurement) square cake pan with baking paper, allowing the sides to overhang.

2 For the chocolate base, combine the flours, sugar and cocoa in a large bowl. Add the butter and stir until well combined. Press chocolate mixture over the base of the prepared pan and bake for 15 minutes or until firm to touch.

3 Reduce oven temperature to 160°C/140°C fan forced. Place the white chocolate and butter in a heatproof bowl over a saucepan of simmering water (don't let the water touch the bowl). Stir until the mixture is melted and smooth. Set aside to cool slightly.

4 Add eggs and flour to the cooled chocolate mixture and whisk until well combined. Divide into 2 portions. Add caster sugar to 1 portion. Mix until well combined. Add brown sugar and golden syrup to the remaining portion and mix until well combined. Spoon heaped spoonfuls of the mixture, alternating between portions, onto the chocolate base. Bake for 1 hour 10 minutes or until a skewer inserted into the centre of slice comes out slightly sticky. Set aside to cool completely in the pan.

5 Place milk chocolate and oil in a microwave-safe bowl. Microwave, stirring every 30 seconds, on high for 1½ minutes or until smooth. Spread evenly over slice. Sprinkle with the crushed biscuits. Place in the fridge for 1 hour to set.

6 Meanwhile, hold 1 Golden Gaytime firmly and pull to remove the stick. Repeat with remaining Gaytimes. Arrange, overlapping, in a 9.5 x 19.5cm loaf pan. Press to seal edges together. Freeze for 2 hours or until firm.

7 Cut the slice into squares and serve topped with scoops of the Gaytime ice-cream. Drizzle with the caramel sauce.

○ GLUTEN FREE ● MAKE AHEAD ● FREEZABLE ● KID FRIENDLY ● EASY

STEP-BY-STEP
HOW-TO GUIDE

Get the expert step-by-step tips to recreate this devilishly irresistible slice.

1 Line the pan with paper overhanging so the slice is easy to lift out. After pressing the base into the pan, go over it with a flat-sided glass to smooth any finger marks.

2 When you add the golden syrup and brown sugar to 1 portion and the caster sugar to the other, the mixtures may look oily, but will cook beautifully.

3 Alternating spoonfuls of batter, overlapping, creates a lovely two-toned rippled effect. Make sure to use all the batter – you might need two layers.

4 Make sure the slice is cooled completely in the pan before pouring over the chocolate. This helps the chocolate to set faster.

5 Bigger chunks will give you a better 'Gaytime' effect, so place the crushed biscuits in a fine sieve over a bowl to remove smaller crumbs.

6 When you make the ice-cream, make sure the Gaytimes are still a bit firm, and press them together firmly to create a solid block.

BROWNIE CHEESECAKE STACK

Stack rich layers of fudgy brownie with creamy cheesecake for the ultimate slice, all topped with stunning chocolate flowers!

SERVES 9 **PREP** 45 mins (+ cooling & overnight chilling) **COOK** 35 mins

200g dark chocolate, finely chopped
180g unsalted butter, chopped
1 tsp vanilla extract
6 eggs
255g (1¼ cups, firmly packed)
   brown sugar
100g (1 cup) hazelnut meal
75g (½ cup) plain flour
35g (⅓ cup) cocoa powder
Chocolate flowers, to decorate
   (see recipe, page 128)

CHEESECAKE FILLING
375g cream cheese,
   at room temperature
45g (¼ cup) icing sugar mixture
200g white cooking chocolate,
   melted, cooled
300ml thickened cream, whipped
1 tbs icing sugar mixture, extra
250g fresh raspberries
Pink food colouring, to tint (optional)
2½ tbs warm water
3½ tsp gelatine powder

DARK CHOCOLATE GANACHE
100ml pouring cream
140g dark chocolate melts

1 Preheat oven to 170°C/150°C fan forced. Lightly grease three 20cm (base measurement) square cake pans with oil. Line the base and sides with baking paper, allowing the sides to overhang.

2 Melt chocolate and butter in a heatproof bowl over a saucepan of simmering water (don't let the water touch the bowl), stirring with a metal spoon until smooth. Stir in the vanilla.

3 Separate 3 eggs, placing the yolks and egg whites in separate bowls. Use electric beaters to beat the sugar, yolks and remaining eggs in a bowl for 2 minutes or until thick and creamy. Stir in the melted chocolate mixture. Fold in the hazelnut meal, flour and cocoa until well combined.

4 Use clean electric beaters to beat the egg whites in a bowl until soft peaks form. Use a large metal spoon to fold the egg whites into the chocolate mixture. Divide mixture evenly among the prepared pans. Bake for 15-20 minutes or until a skewer inserted in the centre comes out clean. Cool completely.

5 Lightly grease a 20cm (base measurement) square cake pan with oil. Line the base and sides with plastic wrap, allowing sides to overhang. Place 1 of the brownies in the pan.

6 For the cheesecake filling, use electric beaters to beat cream cheese and icing sugar in a bowl until smooth. Beat in the melted white chocolate and fold in one-third of the whipped cream. Repeat in 2 more batches. Divide mixture in half.

7 Process extra icing sugar and half the raspberries in a food processor until smooth. Strain through a fine sieve. Discard seeds. Fold into 1 portion of the cream cheese mixture, adding a few drops of food colouring, if desired.

8 Place 1½ tbs warm water in a small bowl. Sprinkle over 2 tsp gelatine. Stir until combined. Place the bowl in a larger bowl half filled with boiling water. Stir for 1 minute or until the gelatine dissolves. Set aside for 1 minute to cool slightly. Fold into the raspberry cream cheese mixture. Pour over the brownie layer in the cake pan and smooth the surface. Top with another brownie layer, pressing down lightly to secure.

○ GLUTEN FREE ● **MAKE AHEAD** ○ FREEZABLE ○ KID FRIENDLY ○ EASY

9 Repeat to dissolve remaining gelatine in the remaining warm water. Set aside for 1 minute to cool slightly. Fold into the remaining cream cheese mixture. Pour over the brownie layer in the pan. Top with remaining raspberries and press into the mixture. Smooth the surface. Top with the remaining brownie. Press lightly to secure. Cover with plastic wrap and place in the fridge for 7 hours or overnight until set.

10 For the dark chocolate ganache, place the cream and chocolate in a small saucepan over low heat and cook, stirring, for 3-5 minutes or until chocolate has melted and ganache mixture is smooth. Set aside to cool and thicken slightly.

11 Drizzle cake with the chocolate ganache and top with chocolate flowers.

STEP-BY-STEP
HOW-TO GUIDE

Make these beautiful chocolate flowers to top your brownie stack.

  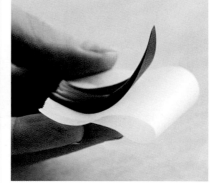

1 Dip a small knife into 375g melted dark choc melts. Tap to remove any excess. Wipe on baking paper, pulling towards you to make the petal.

2 Carefully transfer the chocolate petals on their baking paper to curved patty pans and set aside for 5 minutes to set.

3 Gently peel the paper away from the chocolate petals. Place the remaining melted chocolate in a small piping bag.

4 Place cotton wool in a dish to hold the petals. Overlap 5 petals in dish, securing with melted chocolate. Repeat with 3-5 more petals inside.

5 Use a small paint brush to brush a Malteser all over with edible gold lustre powder to coat (available at specialty baking stores).

6 Use a small amount of chocolate to secure the gold Malteser in centre of chocolate flower. Set aside for 10 minutes for the flower to set.

★★★★★

This worked a treat! I loved the lightness of the mousse in between the brownie layers.

BROOKETHEBAKER

JAFFA CHOCOLATE
CHEESECAKE

Chocolate and cream cheese collide in this dreamy
choc-orange cheesecake topped with bright crunchy Jaffas.

SERVES 12 **PREP** 30 mins (+ chilling & cooling) **COOK** 1 hour 10 mins

125g butter, melted, plus extra,
   to grease
250g pkt plain chocolate biscuits,
   broken into pieces
1 tsp finely grated orange rind
200g dark cooking chocolate,
   finely chopped
2 x 250g pkts cream cheese,
   at room temperature
300g ctn sour cream
155g (¾ cup) caster sugar
2 tbs cocoa powder, sifted
3 eggs
340g pkt Jaffas, to decorate
CHOCOLATE GANACHE
100g dark cooking chocolate,
   finely chopped
125ml (½ cup) thickened cream

1 Invert the base of a 22cm springform pan. Grease and line the base with baking paper. Secure base back in the pan.

2 Place the biscuit and orange rind in a food processor. Process until finely crushed. Add the butter. Process until well combined. Transfer to the prepared pan. Use a straight-sided glass to firmly press mixture over the base and side of the pan, leaving the top 2cm of the pan free. Cover with plastic wrap and place in the fridge for 30 minutes to chill.

3 Preheat oven to 160°C/140°C fan forced. Place the chocolate in a microwave-safe bowl. Microwave on Medium, stirring every minute, for 3-5 minutes or until melted and smooth.

4 Place the cream cheese, sour cream and sugar in a clean food processor. Process until smooth and well combined. Add the cocoa and eggs, and process until well combined. With the motor running, gradually add the melted chocolate and process until well combined.

5 Pour mixture into the biscuit crust and smooth the surface. Bake for 1 hour or until just set in the centre. Turn oven off. Leave in the oven, with the door ajar, for 2 hours or until cooled to room temperature (this will prevent the cheesecake from cracking). Cover and place in the fridge for 4 hours to chill.

6 To make the ganache, place the chocolate and cream in a microwave-safe bowl. Microwave, stirring every minute, for 3-5 minutes or until melted.

7 Pour the ganache over the top of the cheesecake. Use a small palette knife to smooth the surface. Place in the fridge for 15 minutes to firm up slightly. Decorate the top with Jaffas, in circles from outside edge to centre, to serve.

○ GLUTEN FREE ○ MAKE AHEAD ○ FREEZABLE ○ KID FRIENDLY ● EASY

★★★★★ *Sooo decadent, and I love how we all got Jaffas to roll around in our mouths!* **SHAWNSALAD**

30 minutes prep

STEP-BY-STEP
HOW-TO GUIDE

Follow these tips for a crunchy base and a smooth chocolate cheesecake.

1 Invert the base of your pan so that the top is completely flat. This allows you to easily slide your finished cheesecake off the base and remove the baking paper.

2 Use a straight-sided glass to press the biscuit mixture over the base and side of the pan. This will help you achieve a smooth and even crust on your cheesecake.

3 When you're melting chocolate in the microwave, heat the chocolate in small bursts of 1 minute, and use a metal spoon for stirring. This will stop the chocolate from seizing.

4 For the best cheesecake texture – smooth and creamy – make sure that your cream cheese has reached room temperature before you place it in the food processor.

5 Adding the melted chocolate to the food processor while the motor is still running ensures the chocolate is well incorporated into the cream cheese mixture before it sets.

6 Once you pour the chocolate ganache over your chilled cheesecake, use a small palette knife to spread it over the filling. This will help you to achieve a smooth and even layer.

★★★★★ *This was surprisingly easy to make — only half an hour to prep — and the choc-orange flavours are divine!* **CURLYSHIRLEY**

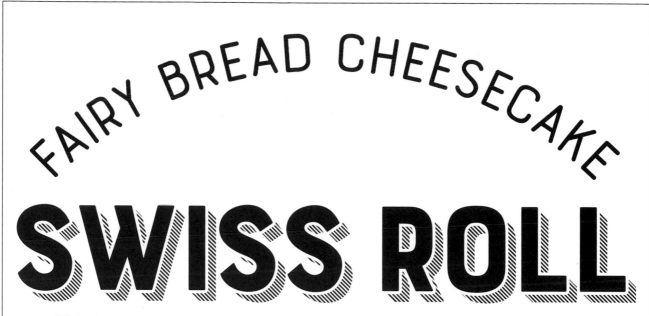

FAIRY BREAD CHEESECAKE SWISS ROLL

This fairy bread-inspired Swiss roll, starring cubes of jelly and creamy cheesecake, is a party on a plate!

SERVES 8 **PREP** 30 mins (+ cooling & 3 hours setting) **COOK** 15 mins

400ml boiling water
85g pkt lime jelly crystals
85g pkt creaming soda jelly crystals
4 eggs, separated
140g (⅔ cup) caster sugar
1 tsp vanilla extract
75g (½ cup) plain flour
60g (½ cup) rainbow sprinkles

CHEESECAKE JELLY FILLING
250g pkt cream cheese, chopped,
   at room temperature
50g butter, at room temperature
1 tsp vanilla extract
80g (½ cup) icing sugar mixture

1 Pour 200ml boiling water into a heatproof jug. Stir in the lime jelly crystals until dissolved. Pour into a 13cm square airtight container. Place in the fridge for 3 hours or until set. Repeat with the creaming soda jelly crystals and remaining boiling water.

2 Preheat oven to 180°C/160°C fan forced. Brush a 24 x 30cm Swiss roll pan with melted butter and line with baking paper.

3 Use electric beaters to beat the egg yolks, sugar and vanilla in a bowl until a ribbon trail forms when the beaters are lifted. Use clean beaters to beat the egg whites in a clean, dry bowl until soft peaks form. Fold into yolk mixture. Sift over flour and use a metal spoon to gently fold until combined. Pour into prepared pan. Smooth surface. Bake for 15 minutes or until a skewer inserted into the centre comes out clean. Cover with baking paper then a damp tea towel and set aside.

4 Place a clean tea towel on a flat work surface. Top with a sheet of baking paper. Cover with sprinkles. Turn out warm cake onto sprinkles. Peel away the paper from base of cake. Starting from 1 long side, roll up the warm cake. Set aside, seam side down, for 20 minutes or until almost cooled. Gently unroll cake. Set aside to cool completely.

5 For the cheesecake filling, use electric beaters to beat the cream cheese, butter and vanilla in a bowl until smooth and well combined. Gradually beat in the icing sugar until fluffy.

6 Cut jelly into 2cm cubes. Spoon ⅓ cup cheesecake mixture into a piping bag with a fluted nozzle. Evenly spread cake with remaining cheesecake mixture, leaving a 2cm border. Top with 12-14 cubes of each jelly flavour. Roll up the cake to enclose the filling. Transfer to a serving plate, seam side down. Pipe reserved cheesecake mixture along the top. Decorate with remaining jelly cubes. Serve.

○ GLUTEN FREE ○ MAKE AHEAD ○ FREEZABLE ● KID FRIENDLY ○ EASY

STEP-BY-STEP
HOW-TO GUIDE

Learn our top tips for this gorgeous colourful cake!

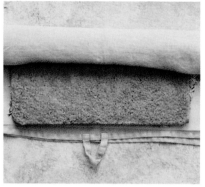

1 After baking, cover the cake with a piece of baking paper, then a damp tea towel. This helps to start the cooling process while keeping it moist to stop it cracking as you roll.

2 When placing the sprinkles on the baking paper, spread them out to the same size as the cake, and as evenly as possible, so that you get an even coating on the cake.

3 Starting from 1 long side, use the tea towel to help you gently roll up the warm cake and stop it cracking. This initial roll will make it easier to roll the cake after it is filled.

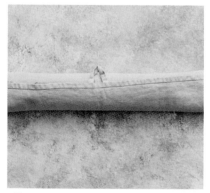

4 Allowing the cake to cool while it is rolled up ensures that once the cake is unrolled and filled with cheesecake mixture and jelly cubes, it will roll up again without cracking.

5 As you spread the remaining cheesecake mixture evenly over the cake, it is important to leave a 2cm border. This will prevent the filling oozing out when you roll it up.

6 Evenly space out the 12-14 lime and 12-14 creaming soda jelly cubes over the cheesecake mixture layer. This will help ensure the cake rolls up evenly.

★★★★★ *I made this for my niece's 6th birthday and cemented my favourite aunty status – winner!* **CLAIREBEAR878**

FLAKE CAKE WITH SWIRLS

With dark, milk and white chocolate layers, this luxuriously stacked chocolate cake features twists, swirls and curls!

SERVES 14 **PREP** 45 mins (+ cooling & chilling) **COOK** 1 hour 40 mins

40g dark chocolate, finely chopped
430g (2 cups) caster sugar
250ml (1 cup) milk
150g butter
225g (1½ cups) self-raising flour
190g (1¼ cups) plain flour
50g (½ cup) cocoa powder
3 x ⅛ tsp bicarbonate of soda
3 eggs
40g milk chocolate, finely chopped
40g white chocolate, finely chopped
2 tsp vanilla extract
Chocolate curls, to decorate
   (see Steps 1-2, page 140)

CHOCOLATE BUTTERCREAM
375g unsalted butter,
   at room temperature
750g (5 cups) icing sugar mixture
2 tbs milk
200g dark chocolate, melted, cooled
200g milk chocolate, melted, cooled
2 x 30g pkts Cadbury Flake,
   crumbled

1 Preheat oven to 180°C/160°C fan forced. Grease a round 19cm (base measurement) cake pan with melted butter and line the base with baking paper.

2 For the dark chocolate cake, place the dark chocolate, ⅔ cup caster sugar, ⅓ cup milk and 50g butter in a large saucepan. Cook over low heat, stirring, for 2-3 minutes or until smooth (do not boil). Set aside for 5 minutes to cool slightly.

3 Whisk in ½ cup self-raising flour, ¼ cup plain flour, ⅓ cup cocoa powder, ⅛ tsp bicarb and 1 egg until well combined. Spoon into prepared pan. Bake for 25-30 minutes or until a skewer inserted in the centre comes out clean. Cool in the pan for 10 minutes, then transfer to a wire rack to cool completely.

4 For the milk chocolate cake, clean and reline the cake pan. Place the milk chocolate, ⅔ cup caster sugar, ⅓ cup milk and 50g butter in a saucepan. Cook over low heat, stirring, for 2-3 minutes or until smooth (do not boil). Set aside for 5 minutes to cool slightly.

5 Whisk in ½ cup self-raising flour, ½ cup plain flour, remaining cocoa powder, ⅛ tsp bicarb and 1 egg until combined. Spoon into the prepared pan. Bake for 25-30 minutes or until a skewer inserted in the centre comes out clean. Cool in the pan for 10 minutes, then transfer to a wire rack to cool completely.

6 For the white chocolate cake, clean and reline the cake pan. Place the white chocolate, ⅔ cup caster sugar, ⅓ cup milk and 50g butter in a saucepan. Cook over low heat, stirring, for 2-3 minutes or until smooth (do not boil). Set aside for 5 minutes to cool slightly.

7 Whisk in ½ cup self-raising flour, ½ cup plain flour, ⅛ tsp bicarb, 1 egg and the vanilla extract until well combined. Spoon into the prepared pan. Bake for 25-30 minutes or until a skewer inserted in the centre comes out clean. Cool in the pan for 10 minutes, then transfer to a wire rack to cool completely.

8 For the chocolate buttercream, use electric beaters to beat the butter in a bowl until pale and creamy. Gradually add icing sugar. Beat until combined. Beat in milk until light and creamy. Beat in the melted chocolates until combined. Spoon 1½ cups buttercream into a bowl. Add the flake. Stir to combine.

○ GLUTEN FREE ○ MAKE AHEAD ○ FREEZABLE ● KID FRIENDLY ○ EASY

9 Place the dark chocolate cake on a cake stand or serving plate. Spread top with half the flake buttercream. Top with milk chocolate cake and spread top with remaining flake buttercream. Top with the white chocolate cake.

10 Spread top and side of cake with a thin layer of plain buttercream. Place in fridge for 30 minutes to set.

11 Place the remaining plain buttercream in a piping bag fitted with a petal piping tip. Use a ruler to mark 2.5cm-wide stripes in the buttercream around the side of the cake. Pipe ruffles onto the side of the cake using the ruled lines as a guide. Arrange chocolate curls on top of the cake. Serve.

STEP-BY-STEP
HOW-TO GUIDE

Luscious buttercream and glam chocolate curls make this cake a stunner.

1 To make the chocolate curls, spread 375g melted dark choc melts onto 20 strips of 4 x 11cm baking paper, leaving 1cm of paper exposed.

2 Bend the paper to make a ruffle and secure with a paper clip. Refrigerate until set. Repeat with milk choc melts. Carefully peel away paper.

3 Use a measuring cup for the flake buttercream. This ensures you'll see perfect layers between the cakes when slicing.

4 For a professional finish, coat the outside of the cake with a thin layer of buttercream and fill in any holes between the layers.

5 Use a ruler to measure and mark even lines up the side of the cake before piping. This will act as a guide to pipe the ruffles.

6 With wide end of the nozzle almost touching the cake, pipe ruffles up the side by moving the nozzle back and forth along the lines.

★★★★★ *I made this for a family celebration — absolutely fabulous. Its definitely one for the chocoholics!* **FRIDGETUNER**

CHOC-CARAMEL POPCORN CAKE

Caramel, popcorn and peanut butter come together in this truly spectacular three-tiered birthday cake. This will keep any sweet tooth happy!

SERVES 16   **PREP** 1 hour (+ cooling & chilling)   **COOK** 1 hour 5 mins

450g (3 cups) self-raising flour
50g (⅓ cup) plain flour
240g (1½ cups, lightly packed) brown sugar
85g (¾ cup) almond meal
1½ tsp bicarbonate of soda
300g butter, melted
80ml (⅓ cup) milk
5 eggs
380g can Caramel Top 'n' Fill, whisked until smooth
60ml (¼ cup) pouring cream
1 tbs liquid glucose
Jersey caramels, thinly sliced, to decorate
Lindt Lindor Sea Salt Caramel balls, dark Maltesers and mini waffles, to decorate

PEANUT BUTTER FROSTING
350g butter, chopped, at room temperature
300g (2 cups) icing sugar mixture
90g (⅓ cup) smooth peanut butter

CARAMEL POPCORN
175g pkt Lolly Gobble Bliss Bombs
140g (⅔ cup) caster sugar
60ml (¼ cup) thickened cream

1 Preheat the oven to 170°C/150°C fan forced. Grease the base and side of three 20cm (base measurement) round cake pans and line with baking paper.

2 Combine flours, brown sugar, almond meal and bicarb in a large bowl. Make a well in the centre. Add butter, milk and eggs. Whisk to combine. Divide evenly among prepared pans. Bake for 35 minutes or until golden and a skewer inserted in centre of each cake comes out clean. Transfer pans to a wire rack to cool.

3 For the frosting, use electric beaters to beat butter in a bowl until pale and creamy. Gradually add sugar, beating well. Add peanut butter. Beat until smooth.

4 For the caramel popcorn, line a baking tray with baking paper. Place bliss bombs in a large heatproof bowl. Place sugar in a non-stick frying pan over medium heat. Cook, shaking pan often, for 8-10 minutes until melted and a golden caramel forms. Quickly and carefully add the cream (be careful as the mixture may spit). Stir over low heat until smooth. Bring to the boil. Simmer for 3-4 minutes until bubbling. Remove from the heat and let the bubbles subside. Working quickly, pour over the bliss bombs and stir to combine. Spread over the prepared tray. Set aside to cool.

5 Place 1 cake on a serving plate. Spread one-fifth of the frosting over the top. Reserve ½ cup caramel. Dollop half the remaining caramel randomly over frosting. Top with another cake. Spread one-quarter of the remaining frosting over the top and dollop with remaining caramel. Top with the last cake. Spread remaining frosting over the top and side. Place in the fridge until frosting is firm.

6 Place cream, glucose and reserved caramel in a small saucepan over medium-low heat. Cook, stirring constantly, for 10-15 minutes or until dark golden and thickened (don't let mixture catch on base of pan). Remove from heat. Set aside, stirring often, to cool to room temperature.

7 Pour the caramel sauce over the top of the cake, carefully spreading to the edges and allowing it to drip down the side. Decorate the cake with the caramel popcorn, sliced caramels, Lindor balls, Maltesers and waffles.

○ GLUTEN FREE   ● MAKE AHEAD   ○ FREEZABLE   ● KID FRIENDLY   ○ EASY

STEP-BY-STEP
HOW-TO GUIDE

Follow these steps to perfectly decorate your layer cake.

1 Use the back of a spoon to create indents on each layer of frosting. Spoon caramel in the indents, so that when you cut the cake, there will be hidden pockets of caramel.

2 Use a large palette knife to press the frosting into the layers on the side of the cake. Make sure you completely coat the outside so it's evenly covered from top to bottom.

3 A clever way to get a smooth, flat finish on your frosting is to lightly scrape it with the removable metal base of a straight-sided tart tin. Do the sides first and then smooth the top.

4 To get a sharp edge on the top of the cake, chill the iced cake until the frosting is firm. Then, use a small sharp knife to trim off any overhanging frosting along the edges.

5 Work quickly when spreading the caramel sauce, as the chilled cake will set it. Use the back of a spoon to smooth the surface and push small amounts over the side of the cake.

6 When pouring the caramel over the popcorn, work quickly to prevent it all sticking together. Stir, then spread over the lined tray. When cool enough to handle, break into pieces.

★★★★★ *This was really fun to make and so yummy, well worth the effort.* **BACONANDEGGS47**

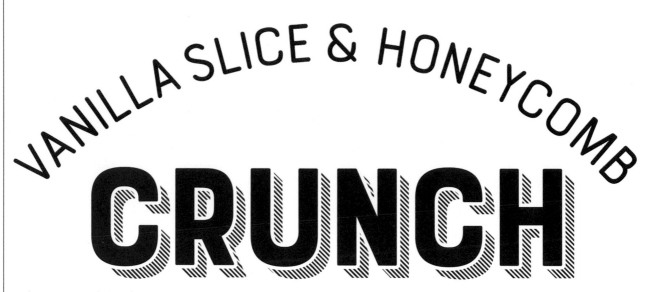

VANILLA SLICE & HONEYCOMB CRUNCH

Layers of flaky, buttery pastry, creamy custard filling with toffee macadamias, honeycomb and caramel on top are ready to impress!

MAKES 12 slices **PREP** 30 mins (+ cooling & 4 hours chilling) **COOK** 50 mins

2 sheets good-quality frozen butter
   puff pastry, just thawed
375ml (1½ cups) pouring cream
170g (¾ cup) caster sugar
1 tsp vanilla extract
40g unsalted butter
375ml (1½ cups) milk
35g (¼ cup) cornflour
6 egg yolks
Pistachio honeycomb, to decorate
   (see page 148)
Toffee macadamias, to decorate
   (see page 148)
Honey, to drizzle

CARAMEL SAUCE
140g (⅔ cup) caster sugar
80ml (⅓ cup) pouring cream

1 Preheat oven to 220°C/200°C fan forced. Line a baking tray with baking paper. Place 1 pastry sheet on the prepared tray. Top pastry with another sheet of baking paper and another baking tray on top. Bake for 15 minutes or until golden and cooked through. Set aside to cool completely. Repeat with remaining pastry sheet.

2 Line the base and sides of a 22cm square cake pan with baking paper, allowing the paper to overhang 2cm above the sides. Place 1 pastry sheet in base of prepared pan, trimming to fit.

3 Place the cream, sugar, vanilla, butter and 250ml (1 cup) milk in a large saucepan. Heat over medium heat until the mixture almost comes to the boil. Remove from the heat.

4 Combine cornflour, egg yolks and remaining milk in a jug. Gradually whisk the egg mixture into the cream mixture until well combined. Return the mixture to medium-low heat and cook, stirring constantly, for 5-10 minutes or until the custard thickens and comes to the boil. Spoon the hot custard over the pastry and smooth the surface. Top with the remaining pastry sheet, trimming to fit. Cover and place in the fridge for 4 hours or overnight to set.

5 To make the caramel sauce, stir the sugar and 80ml (⅓ cup) water in a saucepan over low heat until the sugar dissolves. Simmer for 8 minutes or until golden. Reduce the heat to low and carefully whisk in the cream until combined (be careful as it may spit).

6 Coarsely chop the pistachio honeycomb. Cut the vanilla slice into 12 pieces. Top with the chopped honeycomb and toffee macadamias. Drizzle over the caramel sauce and honey to serve.

○ GLUTEN FREE   ● MAKE AHEAD   ○ FREEZABLE   ○ KID FRIENDLY   ○ EASY

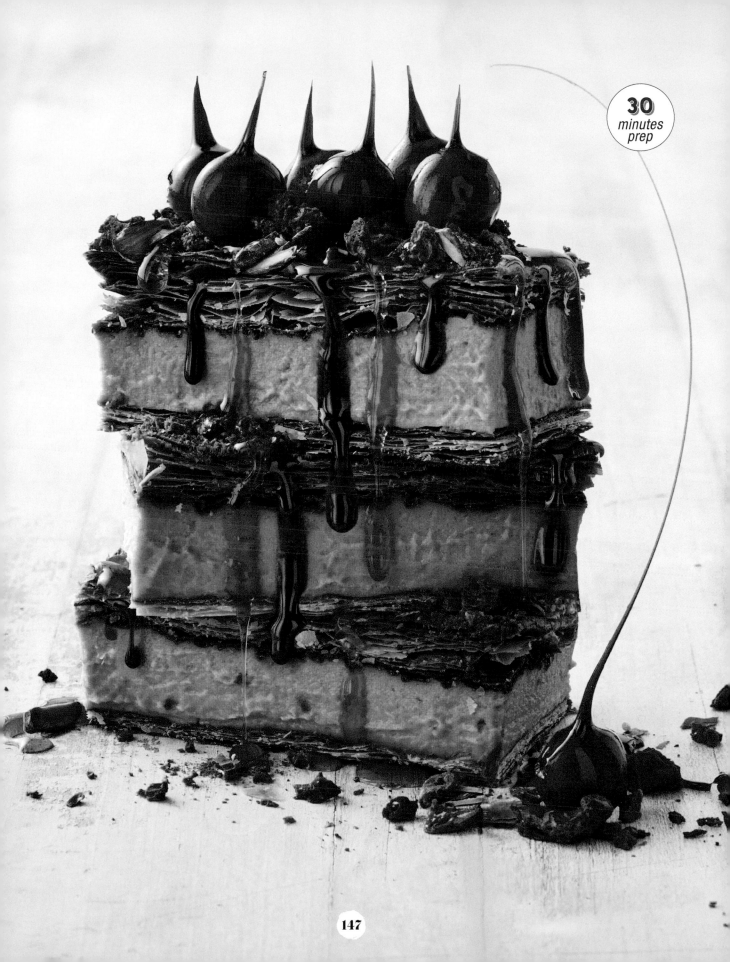

STEP-BY-STEP
HOW-TO GUIDE

Dial up your vanilla slice with honeycomb and toffee macadamias

PISTACHIO HONEYCOMB

1 Place 335g white sugar, 125ml water, 60ml glucose syrup and 2 tbs golden syrup in a saucepan over low heat. Cook, stirring, for 5-8 minutes until sugar dissolves. Increase heat to high.

2 Bring to boil. Cook, without stirring, for 5-7 minutes until hard crack stage (153°C) on cook's thermometer. Remove from heat. Let bubbles subside. Stir in 2 tsp sifted bicarb with wooden spoon.

3 Pour the mixture into a baking paper-lined roasting pan with paper overhanging the sides. Quickly scatter over 55g coarsely chopped pistachio kernels. Set aside to cool completely.

TOFFEE MACADAMIAS

1 Line a large baking tray with baking paper then place a wire rack over the tray. Individually pierce 145g whole macadamias with toothpicks. Have them all ready before starting toffee.

2 Place 215g caster sugar and 60ml water in a saucepan over low heat. Stir to dissolve. Brush down side with wet pastry brush. Increase heat to medium. Cook, without stirring, until golden.

3 Dip macadamias into toffee. Turn to coat, allowing excess to drip off. Once toffee drip creates a thin string, insert toothpick through rack so it hangs over edge, allowing excess to drip onto paper.

★★★★★

I love a simple vanilla slice, but this makes it super special.

FOODSLED

HAZELNUT & COFFEE DACQUOISE

With layers of nutty meringue and rich whipped filling, the classic French cake dacquoise – pronounced dah-kwahz – is so impressive.

SERVES 10 **PREP** 20 mins (+ cooling & chilling) **COOK** 1 hour 45 mins

85g (¾ cup) hazelnut meal
85g (¾ cup) almond meal
6 egg whites
315g (1½ cups) caster sugar
½ teaspoon cream of tartar
FILLING
60ml (¼ cup) warmed milk
2 tablespoons instant coffee
375g unsalted butter, at room
   temperature
570g (3⅔ cup) icing sugar mixture
CHOCOLATE GLAZE
200g dark chocolate
1 tablespoon glucose syrup
250ml (1 cup) thickened cream

1 Preheat oven to 120°C. Draw an 18cm circle on 2 sheets of baking paper. Use to line 2 baking trays, ink-side down.

2 Combine the hazelnut meal and almond meal in a bowl. Use electric beaters to whisk half the egg whites in a clean, dry bowl until soft peaks form. Gradually add half the sugar, 1 tablespoon at a time, until the sugar dissolves. Use a large metal spoon to gently fold in half the cream of tartar and half the nut meal.

3 Spoon mixture into a piping bag fitted with a 1.5cm nozzle. Pipe in a coil motion onto the prepared trays to make 2 discs. Bake for 50 minutes. Turn off oven. Leave meringue in oven, with the door closed, to cool completely. Repeat with remaining ingredients to make 2 more discs.

4 For the filling, stir the milk and coffee in a bowl until coffee dissolves. Use electric beaters to beat the butter in a large bowl until pale and creamy. Gradually beat in the icing sugar until combined. Gradually beat in milk mixture until light and fluffy. Spoon buttercream into a piping bag fitted with a 1cm round nozzle. Starting from the centre of 1 meringue disc, pipe in a coil motion to cover. Top with another disc. Continue piping and layering, finishing with meringue.

5 Use a small sharp knife to trim the side of the meringue layers. Use a palette knife to spread the remaining buttercream over the top and side of the cake to cover completely and smooth the surface. Place in the fridge for 1 hour to set.

6 For the chocolate glaze, place the cake on a wire rack over a baking tray. Place the chocolate and glucose syrup in a heatproof bowl. Place cream in a saucepan over medium heat and bring almost to the boil. Pour over chocolate mixture. Stand. Stir until combined and smooth.

7 Pour the chocolate glaze over the cake. Use a palette knife to spread evenly, tapping the wire rack carefully a few times to help smooth out the glaze. Set aside for 1 hour to set. Serve.

○ GLUTEN FREE ● MAKE AHEAD ○ FREEZABLE ○ KID FRIENDLY ○ EASY

★★★★★ *This was perfect for an elegant finish to a dinner party. Everyone loved it.* **BAZ23327**

STEP-BY-STEP
HOW-TO GUIDE

Here's all you need to know to create this beautifully-layered dacquoise.

1 Chilled egg whites don't whip very well, so bring your eggs to room temperature before starting. Also make sure your mixer bowl and whisk are completely dry and clean.

2 Using a large metal spoon to fold in the cream of tartar and nut meal helps you to keep as much air as possible in the meringue – be sure to very gently fold together.

3 To pipe the meringue layers, start in the centre of the circle on the baking paper and spiral out in a tight coil. Try to make sure there are no gaps as you go.

4 Make sure to place the cake on a wire rack over a baking tray before spreading with buttercream, otherwise it will be tricky to move onto the rack before adding the chocolate glaze.

5 The heat from the hot cream will melt the chocolate. Stir with a dry metal spoon until smooth. If any water gets into the mixture it may seize and become grainy.

6 After pouring the chocolate glaze over the cake, an offset palette knife is ideal to spread it to a smooth finish, then tapping the wire rack carefully will remove any air bubbles.

★★★★★ *This is a great recipe for both the meringue and the coffee buttercream and have used it multiple times with a few alterations. This is definitely a family favourite and one well worth the time and effort.* **GANAELLE**

ICED VOVO PAVLOVA

This is the ultimate Aussie twist – the colours and flavours of the classic Iced VoVo combined with the iconic pavlova!

SERVES 8-10 **PREP** 30 mins (+ cooling & setting) **COOK** 2 hours 10 mins

6 egg whites, at room temperature
Large pinch cream of tartar
315g (1½ cups) caster sugar
1 tsp vanilla essence
500ml (2 cups) thickened cream
6 Arnott's Iced VoVos, finely crushed
20g (¼ cup) desiccated coconut
115g (⅓ cup) raspberry conserve

MERINGUE PEAKS

2 egg whites, at room temperature
Pinch cream of tartar
100g (½ cup) caster sugar
Wilton Rose Icing Color

PINK MARSHMALLOW

140g (⅔ cup) caster sugar
160ml (⅔ cup) cold water
3 tsp boiling water
3 tsp gelatine powder
Rose food colouring, to tint

1 Preheat oven to 120°C/100°C fan forced. Draw four 18cm circles on 2 sheets of baking paper (4 circles in total). Turn, ink-side down, onto 2 baking trays.

2 Use electric beaters with a whisk attachment to whisk the egg white and cream of tartar in a clean, dry bowl until firm peaks form. Gradually add sugar, 1 tbs at a time, beating constantly until sugar dissolves and mixture is thick and glossy. Beat in vanilla.

3 Divide meringue mixture among the circles. Use a palette knife to carefully spread and shape the meringue until each disc is even. Bake, swapping the trays halfway through cooking, for 1 hour 40 minutes or until the meringues are crisp and dry. Turn oven off. Leave meringues in oven, with the door closed, to cool completely.

4 For the meringue peaks, preheat oven to 120°C/100°C fan forced. Line 2 baking trays with baking paper. Use electric beaters to beat the egg white and cream of tartar in a clean, dry bowl until firm peaks form. Gradually add the sugar, 1 tbs at a time, beating constantly until the sugar dissolves and the mixture is thick and glossy. Carefully stand a piping bag fitted with a 1.5cm nozzle upright in a tall glass. Use a small paintbrush to very lightly paint 4 even stripes of rose food colour into the length of the bag. Carefully spoon the meringue mixture into the piping bag and pipe small peaks onto the prepared trays (the colours will vary the more you pipe). Bake for 30 minutes or until the meringues are crisp and dry. Turn oven off and leave meringues in oven, with door closed, to cool completely.

5 Meanwhile, for the marshmallow, place the sugar and cold water in a small saucepan over medium heat. Cook, stirring, for 2-3 minutes or until the sugar dissolves. Bring to the boil. Reduce heat to medium-low. Simmer for 5-6 minutes or until the syrup thickens slightly. Remove from heat and let bubbles subside. Place the boiling water in a small heatproof bowl. Sprinkle the gelatine over the water and whisk with a fork until well combined. Add to the sugar syrup and stir to combine and dissolve. Set aside for 5 minutes to cool. Transfer to the bowl of an electric mixer with a whisk attachment. Beat on high for 4-5 minutes or until the mixture is fluffy and thickened. Tint with rose food colour.

○ GLUTEN FREE ○ MAKE AHEAD ○ FREEZABLE ● KID FRIENDLY ○ EASY

30 minutes prep

6 Working quickly, spread the marshmallow over 1 of the pavlova discs and top with another pavlova disc. Set aside to set.

7 Use electric beaters to beat the cream until firm peaks form. Combine 1 tbs each of the biscuit and coconut in a bowl. Reserve. Place a plain pavlova disc on a plate or cake stand. Spread with half the jam. Top with a third of the whipped cream. Sprinkle with half the remaining biscuit and half the remaining coconut. Top with the sandwiched marshmallow and pavlova discs. Top with the remaining jam, half the remaining whipped cream and the remaining biscuit and coconut. Top with the remaining pavlova disc and whipped cream. Top with the meringue peaks. Sprinkle with reserved biscuit and coconut mixture.

STEP-BY-STEP
HOW-TO GUIDE

Here are our expert step-by-step tips for creating the perfect layered pavlova.

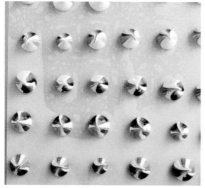

1 To get round, even meringue layers, trace around the circumference of an 18cm plate or bowl onto the baking paper.

2 To see if the sugar has fully dissolved, rub a little meringue between your fingers. It will feel silky-smooth when it's ready.

3 Carefully balance the piping bag in a glass and lightly paint a little of the rose food colour in 4 stripes up the plastic.

4 Pipe slightly different sizes of the meringue peaks onto the trays to ensure you get a range to fit on the top of your cake.

5 The marshmallow is ready when it's thick, fluffy and a ribbon trail forms when the whisk is lifted from the mixture.

6 Use a skewer to add a tiny amount of rose food colour to the marshmallow. Check the colour before adding more – it's highly concentrated!

★★★★★

Tasted like an Iced VoVo but even better. Got a massive tick and left overs were next to nothing.

AMYA101096

BACI STACK WITH FAULT LINE

This epic triple-layered chocolate cake stars a Baci chocolate fault line with a luscious dark chocolate Swiss meringue buttercream finish.

SERVES 20 **PREP** 1 hour 30 mins (+ chilling) **COOK** 50 mins

Melted butter, to grease
450g (3 cups) plain flour
645g (3 cups) caster sugar
90g (¾ cup) cocoa powder
3 tsp bicarbonate of soda
1½ tsp baking powder
1 tsp salt
3 eggs
375ml (1½ cups) buttermilk
375ml (1½ cups) vegetable oil
375ml (1½ cups) hot water
2 tsp vanilla extract
4 x 125g pkts Baci Perugina Original Dark chocolates, unwrapped
45g (¼ cup) whole roasted hazelnuts, coarsely chopped

BUTTERCREAM
300g bought pasteurised liquid egg whites
500g (2⅓ cups) caster sugar
650g unsalted butter, at room temperature, chopped
180g dark chocolate, melted, cooled slightly
Pinch of salt
50g (½ cup) cocoa powder, sifted

1 Preheat oven to 180°C/160°C fan forced. Grease three 20cm (base measurement) round cake pans with melted butter. Line bases and sides with baking paper.

2 Whisk together the flour, sugar, cocoa, bicarb, baking powder and salt in a large bowl. Add the eggs, buttermilk, oil, water and vanilla. Whisk until well combined and smooth. Divide the mixture evenly among the prepared pans. Bake for 45-50 minutes or until a skewer inserted into centre of cake comes out clean. Cool in the pans for 10 minutes, then transfer to a wire rack to cool completely.

3 Meanwhile, for the buttercream, use a stand mixer with the whisk attachment to whisk egg whites and sugar in a large heatproof bowl. Place bowl over a saucepan of simmering water (don't let the water touch the bowl). Cook, stirring often with a whisk, for 3-5 minutes or until hot to touch (to test, transfer a small amount to a saucer. If the mixture is hot, it is ready). Remove from the heat and transfer mixture to a stand mixer with the whisk attachment. Whisk on high speed for 10 minutes or until almost room temperature. Switch to the paddle attachment. On low speed, gradually add the butter, beating well after each addition, until smooth and creamy. Add the melted chocolate and salt. Beat until well combined. Scrape down the bowl. Add cocoa and beat on low speed until combined. Spoon 2 cups of the buttercream into a piping bag fitted with a fluted nozzle and reserve.

4 Use a serrated knife to trim the top of each cake, if needed. Use a little of the buttercream to secure one cake, cut-side up, on a serving platter or board. Spread ½ cup of the buttercream over the top of the cake. Repeat with a second cake layer and ½ cup buttercream. Top with the remaining cake, cut-side down. Spread 2 cups of the chocolate buttercream over the top and sides of the cake to create a crumb coat. Place the cake in the fridge for 20 minutes to chill.

5 Use an offset palette knife to spread a thin layer of remaining buttercream around the middle of the cake, leaving the top third and bottom third of the cake exposed. Reserve 16 whole Baci chocolates and slice remaining Baci into three slices each. Attach slices of Baci to the thin layer of buttercream on the side of the cake, pressing gently.

○ GLUTEN FREE ● MAKE AHEAD ○ FREEZABLE ○ KID FRIENDLY ○ EASY

6 Spoon the remaining buttercream into a piping bag and snip off the end. Pipe around the top and bottom portions on the side of the cake, making sure to keep the middle Baci area uncovered. Use the palette knife to smooth the top and bottom piping on the side, creating the 'fault lines', while being careful not to go over the exposed Baci.

7 Use the reserved butter cream to pipe rosettes around the top edge of the cake. Add a reserved Baci to each rosette. Sprinkle with hazelnuts.

STEP-BY-STEP
HOW-TO GUIDE

Here's how to create the 'fault line' effect on this stunning cake.

1 Adding a thin layer of buttercream to the centre of your cake over the crumb coat allows your Baci to stick flat and keeps them from moving when smoothing out the buttercream.

2 Piping a thick layer of buttercream on the top and bottom of your cake on either side of the Baci, creating a wide exposed layer, makes it easier to make your Baci fault line.

3 To create the perfect sharp edge on the top of your cake, place a 22cm round board on top to use as a guide when you are smoothing out your buttercream on the sides.

4 Once you've smoothed the side of the cake, add additional buttercream into any gaps to refill, and then smooth the side again to remove any excess.

5 After smoothing the side, chill your cake for at least 20 minutes. This will make it easier to remove the board from the top of the cake without taking any of the buttercream with it.

6 If you find your buttercream is getting soft, place the cake in the fridge for 20 minutes before adding the Baci to the top, to create a professional-looking finish.

★★★★★ *Hooley dooley! This cake is crazy, in the best way. I wasn't sure how it would all work, but it did!* **DRAGONRIDER**

CHERRY RIPE CUPCAKES

Topped with buttercream and ganache, these wickedly delicious choc-cherry cupcakes are easy to make and fun to decorate.

MAKES 12 **PREP** 45 mins (+ cooling) **COOK** 30 mins

150g (1 cup) self-raising flour
100g (1 cup) caster sugar
45g (½ cup) desiccated coconut
30g (¼ cup) cocoa powder
150g butter, melted
125ml (½ cup) coconut cream
2 eggs
4 x 52g pkts Cadbury Cherry Ripe,
    chopped into 1cm pieces
12 Mini Oreos
3 x 52g pkts Cadbury Cherry Ripe,
    extra, cut into thick diagonal slices
Freeze-dried strawberries, crushed

CHOCOLATE GANACHE
300g dark chocolate, finely chopped
125ml (½ cup) thickened cream
2 tbs thickened cream, extra

BUTTERCREAM
375g butter, at room temperature
450g (3 cups) icing sugar mixture
1 tbs milk
100g dark chocolate, melted, cooled
2 drops red food colour gel

1 Preheat oven to 180°C/160°C fan forced. Line twelve 100ml muffin pans with 3.5cm deep paper cases.

2 Combine the flour, sugar, coconut and cocoa in a bowl. Make a well in the centre. Add the melted butter, coconut cream and eggs to the well. Use a balloon whisk to whisk until well combined. Stir in the chopped Cherry Ripe. Spoon into the cases. Bake for 25 minutes or until a skewer inserted into the centre comes out clean. Cool in the pan for 10 minutes, then transfer to a wire rack to cool completely.

3 Meanwhile, for the chocolate ganache, place the chocolate and thickened cream in a heatproof bowl. Microwave on High, stirring every minute, for 2 minutes or until melted and smooth. Set aside, stirring occasionally, for 20 minutes or until the mixture thickens slightly.

4 Reserve ½ cup of the ganache in a separate bowl. Carefully spread the remaining ganache over the top of each cake. Set aside to set slightly.

5 For the buttercream, use electric beaters to beat the butter in a bowl until softened. Gradually add the icing sugar, beating until pale and creamy. Add milk and beat until well combined. Transfer half the buttercream to a separate bowl. Add the melted chocolate to one portion and beat until well combined. Add red food gel to the remaining buttercream portion and mix until well combined.

6 Place the chocolate buttercream in a piping bag fitted with a 1.5cm fluted nozzle. Pipe onto the cakes.

7 Place the pink buttercream in a piping bag fitted with a 1.5cm fluted nozzle. Pipe a swirl on top of the chocolate buttercream.

8 Add the extra cream to the reserved ganache and mix to combine. Melt in the microwave on High for 10 seconds or until runny. Place in a piping bag. Set aside for 10 minutes to cool slightly. Top cupcakes with sliced Cherry Ripe and Oreos. Snip the end of the piping bag and drizzle ganache over top of cakes. Sprinkle with crushed strawberry just before serving.

○ GLUTEN FREE ○ MAKE AHEAD ○ FREEZABLE ● KID FRIENDLY ● EASY

★★★★★ *We used ganache in the icing instead of extra chocolate but besides that followed the recipe and it was fantastic.* **RENEETINA**

STEP-BY-STEP
HOW-TO GUIDE

Create perfect layers of ganache and buttercream with our easy tips.

1 Use a spoon to carefully spread the ganache over the top of each cupcake. Set them aside to allow the ganache to set slightly.

2 Use electric beaters to quickly beat in melted chocolate to a portion of buttercream. Beating it in stops the chocolate becoming too hard.

3 Place chocolate buttercream in a piping bag fitted with a 1.5cm fluted nozzle. Pipe a flat swirl onto each ganache-topped cupcake.

4 Adding the drops of food gel to a skewer to add to the buttercream gives you more control over the desired colour outcome. Use a spatula to combine.

5 Place the pink buttercream in a piping bag fitted with a 1.5cm fluted nozzle. Pipe a swirl of the pink buttercream on the cupcake finishing with a peak at the top.

6 Pour the runny ganache into a piping bag or sealable plastic bag. Snip off one corner to make a small hole. Drizzle the ganache over the top of the cupcakes.

★★★★★

*The cupcakes
were divine.
Am making
again next week.*

JACKIEH2203

CHEESECAKE CHOCOLATE BUNDT

Meet the bake of your dreams – a decadent chocolate cake with a creamy cheesecake centre and luxe chocolate glaze.

SERVES 12 **PREP** 20 mins (+ cooling) **COOK** 50 mins

285g (1⅓ cups) caster sugar
100g unsalted butter
160ml (⅔ cup) milk
200g dark chocolate, chopped
150g (1 cup) self-raising flour
115g (¾ cup) plain flour
50g (½ cup) cocoa powder
½ tsp bicarbonate of soda
2 eggs
2 tbs vegetable oil
125ml (½ cup) thickened cream

VANILLA CHEESECAKE
250g cream cheese, chopped,
   at room temperature
55g (¼ cup) caster sugar
1 egg
1 tsp vanilla extract
1 tbs plain flour

1 Preheat oven to 160°C/140°C fan forced. Spray a 24cm (top measurement) 8-cup-capacity bundt pan with oil.

2 Place the sugar, butter, milk and 100g chocolate in a microwave-safe bowl. Microwave on High, stirring every minute, until smooth. Cool for 5 minutes. Sift the self-raising flour, plain flour, cocoa and bicarb over the chocolate mixture. Whisk in the eggs and oil.

3 For the cheesecake, use electric beaters to beat the cream cheese and sugar in a bowl until well combined. Beat in the egg and vanilla, then the flour until combined.

4 Pour two-thirds of the cake mixture into the pan. Spoon cheesecake into a sealable plastic bag. Snip 2cm from a corner. Pipe on top of cake mixture, leaving a 2cm border. Top with the remaining cake mixture. Bake for 45 minutes or until a skewer inserted into centre comes out clean. Set aside in pan for 10 minutes. Transfer to a wire rack to cool.

5 Place the cream and remaining chocolate in a microwave-safe jug. Microwave on High, stirring every minute, until melted and smooth. Drizzle over cake to serve.

COOK'S TIP

You can make this cake on the morning of serving, then drizzle with the glaze to serve.

★★★★★ *The cheesecake in the middle turned out beautifully. My partner loved it so much I'm making the cake again for his birthday. A rich, delicious and surprising cake.* **DORA_SZASZ**

○ GLUTEN FREE ○ MAKE AHEAD ○ FREEZABLE ● KID FRIENDLY ● EASY

STEP-BY-STEP
HOW-TO GUIDE

Fill your chocolate cake with a rich cheesecake centre – here's how!

1 When melting the chocolate mixture for the cake, chop the chocolate into similar-sized pieces, so it melts evenly. Stir every minute and be careful not to overcook.

2 Use a hand-held balloon whisk to stir the dry ingredients, eggs and oil into the chocolate mixture and mix until just combined, with no pockets of flour.

3 Having the cream cheese at room temperature will help you to blend it to a smooth consistency. Using electric beaters will also make this a lot easier.

4 Using a sealable plastic bag with the corner snipped will help you to pipe a nice even amount of cheesecake mixture in the centre of the cake.

5 Gently spoon the remaining one-third chocolate cake mixture on top of the cheesecake mixture, so it is completely enclosed.

6 The chocolate glaze doesn't set, so to prevent a gooey mess, place the cake on a serving plate before drizzling it over the top.

★★★★★ *I was expecting this to be tricky, but it was actually pretty easy and turned out beautifully.* **VIOLAPARMESAN**

LEMON CURD CHEESECAKE PAV

This pavlova cheesecake is a dream come true, with rich creamy layers and fruity bursts of raspberries and passionfruit.

SERVES 8 **PREP** 45 mins (+ cooling, setting & 4 hours chilling) **COOK** 1 hour 40 mins

3 egg whites, at room
   temperature
215g (1 cup) caster sugar
1 tsp cornflour
½ tsp white vinegar
250g frozen raspberries
200g white chocolate melts
185ml (¾ cup) double cream
125ml (½ cup) thickened cream
125g punnet fresh raspberries
2 passionfruit, halved

**LEMON CURD CHEESECAKE
FILLING**
250g cream cheese, at room
   temperature
70g (⅓ cup) caster sugar
2 tbs fresh lemon juice
2 tbs warm water
2 tsp gelatine powder
300ml ctn thickened cream
145g (½ cup) lemon curd

1 Preheat oven to 120°C/100°C fan forced. Grease a 6.5cm deep, 12 x 27cm (base measurement) loaf pan and line with baking paper, extending the paper 2cm above the sides.

2 Use electric beaters with the whisk attachment to whisk egg whites in a clean, dry bowl until firm peaks form. Gradually add ¾ cup sugar, 1 tablespoon at a time, beating constantly, until sugar dissolves and the mixture is thick and glossy. Beat in the cornflour and vinegar. Spoon mixture into the prepared pan. Smooth the surface. Bake for 1 hour 30 minutes or until crisp and dry. Turn off the oven. Leave meringue in oven, with the door closed, to cool completely.

3 For the cheesecake filling, use electric beaters to beat cream cheese and sugar in a bowl until smooth. Beat in lemon juice. Place water in a small heatproof bowl. Sprinkle over gelatine and stir until well combined. Place the small bowl inside a larger heatproof bowl. Pour boiling water into the larger bowl so the water comes halfway up the side of the smaller bowl. Set aside, stirring occasionally, for 5 minutes or until gelatine dissolves. Add gelatine mixture to the filling. Beat until combined.

4 Use clean electric beaters to beat the cream in a bowl until soft peaks form. Fold into the cream cheese mixture. Add lemon curd and fold in lightly to create a swirled effect. Spoon on top of the pavlova base. Smooth the surface. Place in the fridge for 3-4 hours to chill and firm.

5 Meanwhile, place the frozen raspberries in a bowl. Sprinkle with the remaining sugar. Set aside for 2 hours. Use a fork to mash the raspberry mixture. Transfer to a sieve over a bowl. Use the back of a spoon to press as much juice as possible into the bowl. Discard the seeds. Set aside.

6 Line a baking tray with baking paper. Place chocolate in a microwave-safe bowl. Heat on Medium, stirring every 30 seconds, for 2-3 minutes until the chocolate is melted. Drizzle over the prepared tray. Tilt tray so the chocolate runs in different directions. Set aside for 10 minutes to set. Break into large pieces.

7 Use a balloon whisk to whisk creams in a bowl until soft peaks form. Use a spatula to transfer cake to a serving plate. Top with cream, raspberries and chocolate pieces. Drizzle with passionfruit pulp and raspberry sauce. Serve.

○ GLUTEN FREE ● MAKE AHEAD ○ FREEZABLE ● KID FRIENDLY ○ EASY

★★★★★ *Turned out just as it looks in the picture. The taste was so good. Definitely a hit and fairly simple to make. Go on try it!* **BATGIRL**

STEP-BY-STEP
HOW-TO GUIDE

We've got all the advice you need to make this irresistible pavlova cake.

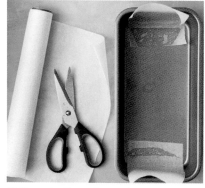

1 To make the cake easier to remove from the pan, cut 2 smaller pieces of baking paper to line the ends and then a larger piece for the centre, all extending 2cm above the sides.

2 For the perfect meringue, make sure that after the sugar is added you continue to beat the mixture until all the sugar has dissolved and the peaks are stiff when the beaters are lifted.

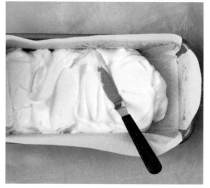

3 For an even pavlova base, spoon the meringue into the prepared pan, then use a palette knife or a flat-bladed knife to spread it evenly over the base and flatten the surface.

4 Gelatine needs to be warmed gently so it doesn't overheat, as this will prevent it setting. Putting the mixture inside a second bowl filled with boiling water is safe and effective.

5 For the perfect lemon curd swirl effect, use a large spoon to gently fold and swirl the curd through the cream cheese mixture. For bursts of curd flavour, don't over-mix.

6 For a seedless raspberry sauce, place the mashed raspberries in a sieve over a bowl. Using a large metal spoon or spatula makes it easier to press out as much juice as possible.

★★★★★
Made this for our Christmas party and everyone loved it especially the lightness of it. Simple to make but does take some time. Worth the effort! **SHELLEYSBELLY**

CHOCOLATE ZEBRA CAKE

Need a real-deal showstopper? Cut into the rich ganache glaze to reveal the dramatic twists and turns of this amazing zebra cake!

SERVES 12   **PREP** 1 hour (+ chilling & setting)   **COOK** 35 mins

6 eggs
370g (1¾ cups) caster sugar
310ml (1¼ cups) milk
250ml (1 cup) vegetable oil
2 tsp vanilla extract
450g (3 cups) self-raising flour
40g (¼ cup) plain flour
30g (¼ cup) dark cocoa, sifted
½ tsp ground cinnamon
60ml (¼ cup) milk, extra
300ml double cream

CHOCOLATE BUTTERCREAM
250g unsalted butter, at room
   temperature
150g (1 cup) icing sugar mixture,
   sifted
180g dark chocolate, melted, cooled

CHOCOLATE GANACHE GLAZE
200g dark chocolate, finely chopped
1½ tbs glucose syrup
200ml pouring cream

ZEBRA CURLS
150g dark choc melts, melted,
   cooled
150g white choc melts, melted,
   cooled

1 Preheat oven to 180°C/160°C fan forced. Grease three 20cm (base measurement) round cake pans and line the base and sides with baking paper.

2 Use electric beaters to beat the eggs and sugar in a bowl for 3 minutes or until pale and creamy. Add the milk, oil and vanilla. Beat until well combined. Add the flours (don't worry if it looks curdled). Stir until well combined.

3 Divide the cake mixture between 2 bowls. Combine the cocoa, cinnamon and extra milk in a bowl to form a paste. Fold the cocoa paste into 1 portion of the cake batter until just combined. Working quickly, drop alternating ¼ cupfuls of plain and chocolate mixture in the centre of the prepared pans to make concentric circles. Bake for 25-30 minutes or until a skewer inserted in the centre comes out clean. Cool in pans for 5 minutes, then transfer to wire racks to cool completely.

4 For the buttercream, use electric beaters to beat the butter and icing sugar in a bowl until pale and creamy. Beat in the chocolate until smooth and combined.

5 Use a serrated knife to trim the tops off the cakes if needed. Place 1 cake on a plate. Spread with ½ cup buttercream. Continue layering with the remaining cakes and buttercream. Spread the remaining buttercream all over the side and top of the cake to coat thinly. Place in the fridge for 1 hour or until firm.

6 For the chocolate ganache glaze, place chocolate and glucose syrup in a heatproof bowl. Place cream in a small saucepan over medium heat. Bring to the boil. Pour over the chocolate mixture. Stir until smooth. Strain through a fine sieve. Set aside for 15 minutes to cool slightly. Place 2 tbs ganache in a separate bowl and reserve.

7 Transfer the cake to a wire cake rack. Place on a baking tray. Pour the ganache over the top and side, allowing any excess ganache to drip off. Place in the fridge for 30 minutes to set. Transfer the cake to a serving plate.

8 For the zebra curls, thinly spread cooled dark chocolate over a marble board or work surface. Drag a cake decorating comb or fork through the chocolate to create even lines. Set aside at room temperature. Spread the cooled white chocolate over the dark chocolate to fill the gaps. Set aside until just set.

○ GLUTEN FREE   ● **MAKE AHEAD**   ○ FREEZABLE   ○ KID FRIENDLY   ○ EASY

9 Using the edge of a sharp knife at a 45° angle, scrape diagonally across the top of the chocolate. If the chocolate has set too hard, leave it in a warm place to soften slightly.

10 Use a balloon whisk to whisk cream until thick enough to dollop. Drizzle over reserved ganache. Fold gently to create a swirled effect. Decorate cake with cream and chocolate curls. Serve.

STEP-BY-STEP
HOW-TO GUIDE

There's no need for guesswork – our tips will guide you through the recipe.

1 To ensure your cake has even zebra rings throughout, use a measuring cup to pour the mixture evenly into each pan, alternating colours.

2 Place each cupful of mixture in the centre of the previous batter. The batter underneath will spread out under the weight.

3 Use a large palette knife to spread the buttercream over the cake for a smooth finish. If you ice a lot of cakes, a cake wheel is very useful for this.

4 Make sure you allow the ganache to cool before pouring it over the buttercream, otherwise the buttercream may melt.

5 For the perfect chocolate zebra curls, use a wide pastry comb to create even lines in the melted dark chocolate.

6 Allow the white choc to cool slightly before pouring over the dark stripes. Spread with a spatula so the top is flat for shaving into curls.

★★★★★
What a cool idea! This needed a bit of concentration and effort, but the final result was A+.

MARBLECAKER11

MALTESER CHEESECAKE SLICE

For a dessert with real wow factor you can't go past this decadent slice layered with a brownie base, white choc centre and dark chocolate topping.

SERVES 16   **PREP** 30 mins (+ 6 hours cooling & setting)   **COOK** 50 mins

100g dark cooking chocolate, chopped
80g butter, chopped
1 egg, lightly whisked
100g (½ cup) caster sugar
100g (⅔ cup) plain flour
2 tbs cocoa powder
1 tbs milk
450g Dark Maltesers
Store-bought chocolate sauce, to drizzle

WHITE CHOC CHEESECAKE
2 tbs hot water
1 tbs gelatine powder
2 x 250g pkts cream cheese, softened
250ml (1 cup) thickened cream
155g (¾ cup) caster sugar
150g white chocolate, melted, cooled
150g Maltesers, roughly chopped

CHOCOLATE GANACHE
150g dark cooking chocolate, chopped
80ml (⅓ cup) thickened cream

1 Preheat oven to 160°C/140°C fan forced. Grease a 6.5cm-deep, 12 x 27cm (base measurement) straight-sided loaf pan and line with baking paper, allowing the long sides to overhang.

2 Place the chocolate and butter in a large microwave-safe bowl. Microwave on High, stirring every minute, for 2-3 minutes or until melted and smooth. Set aside for 5 minutes to cool slightly.

3 Use a balloon whisk to whisk in the egg until combined. Add the sugar, flour, cocoa and milk. Whisk until combined. Stir in 200g Dark Maltesers. Pour the mixture into the prepared pan. Use the back of a spoon to smooth the surface and cover any exposed Maltesers. Bake for 30-40 minutes or until a skewer inserted in the centre comes out clean. Set aside to cool.

4 For the cheesecake, place the hot water in a small heatproof bowl. Sprinkle over the gelatine. Stir until combined. Place the bowl inside a larger heatproof bowl. Add enough boiling water to the large bowl to reach three-quarters of the way up the side of the smaller bowl. Set aside, stirring occasionally, for 5 minutes or until the gelatine dissolves.

5 Meanwhile, process the cream cheese, cream and sugar in a food processor until smooth. Add the melted chocolate and process until well combined.

6 With the motor running, gradually add the gelatine mixture until combined. Transfer to a large bowl. Fold in chopped Maltesers. Spoon into the pan over the cooled chocolate brownie base. Place in the fridge for 6 hours to set.

7 For the ganache, place the chocolate in a heatproof bowl. Heat the cream in a small saucepan over low heat until it just comes to the boil. Pour over the chocolate and set aside for 5 minutes or until the chocolate melts. Stir until combined. Set aside to cool slightly.

8 Pour ganache over the cheesecake to cover. Line the top with the remaining Dark Maltesers. Place in the fridge for 30 minutes to set. Serve drizzled with chocolate sauce.

○ GLUTEN FREE   ● MAKE AHEAD   ○ FREEZABLE   ● KID FRIENDLY   ○ EASY

30
minutes
prep

★★★★★ *Everyone loved the cheesecake and it has been requested multiple times since!* **CLOVERDALE5**

STEP-BY-STEP
HOW-TO GUIDE

Our sneaky tips and tricks will guarantee the perfect finish for your slice.

1 Let the baking paper extend over the longer sides, so they overhang. This will allow you to remove the slice easily. Simply hold the paper on either side and lift it out.

2 It's important not to overheat the gelatine, as this can reduce its ability to set. Placing the mixture in a hot water bath allows the gelatine to dissolve without too much heat.

3 Use a large metal spoon to fold the Maltesers into the cheesecake. We roughly chopped them, but they could be finely chopped for more of a swirled look if you prefer.

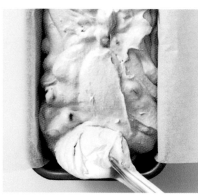

4 After you've spooned the cheesecake into the prepared loaf pan, press it into the sides to fill the pan completely, then smooth the top. Tap the pan on the bench a few times to remove any air pockets.

5 Work quickly when pouring the ganache over the chilled cheesecake, as it will start to set the ganache straight away. Smooth it using an offset palette knife or the back of a spoon.

6 For the top, we sorted through the Maltesers to find ones of similar size, as it was easier to line them up. Neat rows will make the slice easier to cut, as well, as you can just cut between them.

★★★★★ *Anything combining cheesecake and Maltesers has to be a winner in my book. Absolutely love it.* **LOUMAY006**

FESTIVE & FUN

WHEN IT COMES TO CHRISTMAS AND EASTER, IT'S ALWAYS FUN TO MAKE SOMETHING EXTRA SPECIAL TO HAVE PRIDE OF PLACE ON THE TABLE. WITH THESE SENSATIONAL RECIPES, YOU'RE ALL SET FOR A FESTIVE DESSERT TO REMEMBER.

JUMBO ICED VOVO TART

This deliciously fun teatime treat takes inspiration from one of Australia's all-time favourite biscuits. Go on, give it a go!

SERVES 8 **PREP** 30 mins (+ cooling & chilling) **COOK** 10 mins

Canola oil spray, to grease
100g Arnott's Iced VoVo biscuits
150g plain sweet biscuits
130g unsalted butter, melted
400ml thickened cream
2 drops pink food colouring
1 tbs moist coconut flakes

MARSHMALLOW FILLING
150g pink marshmallows
1 tbs milk
2 drops pink food colouring
200ml thickened cream
1 tsp vanilla bean paste

RASPBERRY JELLY
2 gelatine leaves
125g (1 cup) frozen raspberries
80ml (⅓ cup) water
1 tbs caster sugar

1 Grease a 35 x 11cm (base measurement) fluted tart tin, with removable base, with canola oil spray. Process Iced VoVo biscuits and plain biscuits until finely crushed. Add the butter. Process to combine. Use a glass to spread and press the mixture firmly over the base and sides of the prepared tin. Place in the fridge for 1 hour to chill.

2 For the marshmallow filling, stir the marshmallows and milk in a small saucepan over medium-low heat for 3 minutes or until the marshmallows melt and the mixture is smooth. Transfer to a bowl. Stir in food colouring. Set aside, stirring occasionally, for 6 minutes to cool.

3 Use electric beaters to beat the cream and vanilla bean paste in a bowl until firm peaks form. Gently fold half the cream mixture into the marshmallow mixture. Fold in the remaining cream mixture until combined. Spoon over the biscuit base and smooth the surface. Place in the fridge for 2 hours or until firm.

4 Meanwhile, for the raspberry jelly, place the gelatine in a bowl and cover with cold water. Set aside for 6 minutes to soften. Stir the raspberries, water and sugar in a small saucepan over medium-low heat for 1 minute or until sugar dissolves. Bring to a simmer. Cook, stirring occasionally, for 2-3 minutes or until raspberries collapse. Squeeze excess liquid from gelatine leaves and add to the raspberry mixture. Stir until the gelatine dissolves. Strain the gelatine mixture through a fine sieve into a bowl. Discard the seeds. Set aside, stirring occasionally, for 25 minutes to cool.

5 Carefully pour the raspberry jelly over the marshmallow mixture. Smooth the surface. Place in the fridge for 2 hours or until set.

6 Use electric beaters to beat the cream in a bowl until firm peaks form. Stir in the food colouring. Spoon into a piping bag fitted with a 1cm fluted nozzle. Pipe rosettes, in 2 rows, along the 2 long sides of the tart. Sprinkle with the coconut flakes. Serve.

○ GLUTEN FREE ● MAKE AHEAD ○ FREEZABLE ● KID FRIENDLY ○ EASY

STEP-BY-STEP HOW TO GUIDE
Use these pictures to help you get the steps just right!

1 For a compact, even biscuit base, use a flat-sided glass to press the mixture into the tin.

2 For maximum raspberry flavour, use a spoon to press the jelly mixture through the sieve. Discard the seeds.

3 For even rows, pipe the rosettes along each long side first, then repeat to make a second row inside.

CHOCOLATE SPECKLED CAKE

This choc-speckled, nest-topped beauty is set to wow the crowd. Keep it plain for everyday or top it with a chocolate nest and eggs for Easter!

SERVES 12 **PREP** 1 hour (+ cooling & chilling) **COOK** 45 mins

375g unsalted butter, chopped, at room temperature
270g (1¼ cups) caster sugar
4 eggs
2 tsp vanilla extract
300g (2 cups) self-raising flour
75g (½ cup) plain flour
300g ctn sour cream
200g dark cooking chocolate, coarsely grated

BUTTERCREAM
300g unsalted butter, chopped, at room temperature
270g (1¾ cups) icing sugar mixture, sifted
1 tsp vanilla extract
100g white chocolate, melted, cooled
Wilton Cornflower Blue and Teal Icing Color, to tint

SPECKLE MIX
1 tsp cocoa powder
1 tbs vanilla extract

CHOCOLATE GANACHE
150ml thickened cream
100g dark chocolate, chopped

1 Preheat oven to 180°C/160°C fan forced. Grease three 20cm round cake pans with melted butter. Line the bases with baking paper.

2 Use electric beaters to beat the butter and sugar in a bowl until pale and creamy. Add the eggs, 1 at a time, beating well after each addition. Beat in the vanilla extract. Gradually fold in the combined flours and the sour cream, in alternating batches, until the mixture is smooth and combined. Fold in the grated chocolate. Divide evenly among the prepared pans and smooth the surface of each. Bake for 35-40 minutes or until a skewer inserted into the centre of each cake comes out clean. Transfer pans to wire racks to cool for 5 minutes, then turn cakes out onto the wire racks to cool completely.

3 For the buttercream, use electric beaters to beat butter, icing sugar and vanilla in a bowl until pale and creamy. Beat in white chocolate until smooth. Use a skewer to add a little of each food paste and mix well to tint a duck-egg blue.

4 Place 1 cake on a serving board and top with a little buttercream. Continue layering with the remaining cakes and buttercream. Spread a thin layer of the remaining buttercream over the top and side of cake. Place in the fridge for 10 minutes to set. Spread the remaining buttercream over top and side in a thicker layer. Smooth the surface. Place in the fridge for 1 hour, until firm.

5 For the speckle mix, combine cocoa and vanilla in a small bowl. Cover floor and bench with a dropsheet or newspaper. Dip a small, stiff pastry brush or unused paintbrush in speckle mix and flick over cake to create a speckled look. Reserve remaining speckle mix for eggs (see p188). Chill cake in fridge for 15 minutes.

6 For the ganache, bring the cream just to the boil in a small saucepan over low heat. Place chocolate in a small heatproof bowl and pour over the cream. Set aside for 5 minutes. Stir until smooth. Set aside to cool until the consistency of thickened cream. Use a spoon to drizzle the ganache over top of cake, letting it drip down sides. Set aside for 15 minutes to set slightly.

7 Decorate the cake with the noodle nest and choc-speckled eggs (follow our easy step-by-step guide on p188).

○ GLUTEN FREE ● MAKE AHEAD ○ FREEZABLE ● KID FRIENDLY ○ EASY

★★★★★ *Top marks for this cake! I made it for a birthday and left off the nest and eggs – it was delicious!* **DRPRETTY**

STEP-BY-STEP
HOW-TO GUIDE

Make a beautiful bird's nest and eggs to top your chocolate cake!

1 Lightly oil the base of an upturned ceramic or glass cereal bowl and the inside of another bowl. Using your fingers, gently loosen 30g uncooked rice vermicelli noodles. Place in a large bowl.

2 Add 100g melted dark choc melts and use 2 forks to gently toss until the noodles are completely coated (try not to break the noodles). You can use your hands to gently toss the noodles if easier.

3 Shape the chocolate noodles over the base of the greased bowl to form a nest. Place the remaining greased bowl over the top of the nest and press down to shape. Set aside for 20 minutes to set.

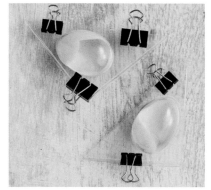

4 You'll need a sheet of 20ml egg moulds and 5ml egg moulds. Cut sheets into individual moulds. Wipe with well-oiled paper towel. Melt 75g white choc melts. Use a skewer to add a little Wilton Cornflour Blue and Teal Icing Color Pastes to the chocolate to tint.

5 Working with two 20ml halves at a time, add 1 tsp melted chocolate to each, secure halves with bulldog clips and turn to fully coat. Repeat with 5ml moulds, adding ½ tsp chocolate to each. Set aside, turning, for 10 minutes to set. Place in the fridge for 5 minutes.

6 Repeat with another 75g choc melts (without tinting) to make more eggs. Remove from moulds. Using reserved speckle mix and a stiff, small pastry brush or unused paintbrush, flick the eggs to decorate. Place on a baking tray in the fridge for 5 minutes to chill.

★ ★ ★ ★ ★

We had a lot of fun making this – the kids especially loved decorating with the chocolate speckle – I recommend newspaper on the floor!

GLAMMA1965

TRADITIONAL HOT CROSS BUNS

Follow our step-by-step guide and surprise friends and family with freshly baked hot cross buns packed with fruit and spices.

MAKES 12 **PREP** 30 mins (+ proving) **COOK** 25 mins

490g (3¼ cups) bread & pizza plain flour, plus extra, to dust
170g (1 cup) sultanas
2 tbs mixed peel
2 tbs caster sugar
1 tsp dried yeast
1 tsp mixed spice
1 tsp ground cinnamon
1 tsp ground nutmeg
Large pinch of salt
250ml (1 cup) warm milk
50g butter, melted, cooled
1 egg, lightly whisked

CROSS PASTE
40g (¼ cup) plain flour
2 tbs cold water

GLAZE
70g (⅓ cup) caster sugar
80ml (⅓ cup) cold water

1 Brush a baking tray with melted butter. Combine the flour, sultanas, mixed peel, sugar, yeast, mixed spice, cinnamon, nutmeg and salt in a large bowl. Stir to combine. Make a well in the centre.

2 Add the milk, butter and egg to the well. Use a wooden spoon to stir until just combined. Use your hands to bring the dough together in the bowl.

3 Turn the dough out onto a well-floured surface. Knead for 10-15 minutes or until smooth and elastic. Brush a large bowl with melted butter. Place dough in the bowl. Turn to coat. Cover and set aside in a warm place to prove for 1½ hours or until doubled in size.

4 Preheat oven to 200°C/180°C fan forced. Punch down dough. Knead on a lightly floured surface for 2-3 minutes, until smooth. Divide into 12 balls. Place on prepared tray. Set aside in a warm place for 30 minutes.

5 For the cross paste, combine the flour and water in a bowl. Transfer to a piping bag fitted with a small nozzle. Pipe lines on the buns to form crosses. Bake for 20 minutes or until golden and hollow when tapped.

6 For the glaze, place the sugar and water in a saucepan over medium heat. Cook, stirring, for 3 minutes or until sugar dissolves and mixture thickens slightly. Brush the tops of the warm buns with the glaze.

COOK'S TIP

If you're using yeast that you've had for a while, test to ensure it's active before starting. Combine yeast, sugar and 125ml (½ cup) of the warm milk in a bowl. Set aside in a warm place for 5 minutes. If it turns frothy, the yeast is active. Add the mixture to the flour mixture with remaining warm milk in Step 2.

○ GLUTEN FREE ○ MAKE AHEAD ● **FREEZABLE** ● **KID FRIENDLY** ○ EASY

★★★★★ *This is the best recipe. Super easy, resulting in that old-fashioned, traditional Easter Bun I remember from my childhood.* **ANNELLAW**

STEP-BY-STEP
HOW-TO GUIDE

Here's how to make your own perfectly glazed hot cross buns.

1 Combine the dry ingredients in a large bowl. Make sure the fruit is well coated in the flour – this stops it sinking to the bottom during baking. Brush the baking tray with butter to prevent sticking.

2 To make the dough, make a well in the dry ingredients and pour in the wet ingredients. Use a wooden spoon to gradually stir until incorporated. This stops lumps of flour forming in the dough.

3 To knead, use your hands to push, fold and turn the dough until smooth and elastic. This helps the buns rise by stretching the gluten strands and working the yeast through the dough.

4 When the dough has doubled in size, punch down the centre with your fist. This removes any air pockets that may have developed in the dough. Knead again, then shape into rolls on the tray.

5 To make crosses, pipe paste onto the buns using a piping bag fitted with a 2mm plain nozzle. To keep the paste flowing and to avoid air bubbles, twist the bag and apply even pressure as you pipe.

6 Brushing the tops with glaze creates finger-licking stickiness and a shiny, professional finish. Make sure the glaze is warm – as it cools it will thicken, so it won't coat the hot cross buns properly.

TWIST IT!

CHOCOLATE-FILLED HOT CROSS BUNS: Omit mixed spice, nutmeg and mixed peel from Traditional Hot Cross Buns recipe. Add 2 tbs cocoa powder to the flour mixture. When forming the dough into buns, place a 10g piece of dark chocolate into the centre of each ball and shape dough around chocolate to enclose. For the cross paste, reduce flour to 2 tbs and add 1 tbs cocoa powder to the mixture. Bake and glaze following Traditional Hot Cross Buns recipe.

WHITE CHRISTMAS LAMINGTONS

These aren't your ordinary lamingtons! Bite into the vanilla sponge and you'll find a crispy cranberry white Christmas surprise inside.

MAKES 15 **PREP** 30 mins (+ cooling & chilling) **COOK** 45 mins

250g butter, at room temperature
215g (1 cup) caster sugar
3 eggs
2 tsp vanilla extract
300g (2 cups) self-raising flour
125ml (½ cup) milk
215g (2½ cups) shredded coconut

WHITE CHRISTMAS
2 x 180g pkt white chocolate, finely chopped
120g dried cranberries, finely chopped
70g (⅔ cup) desiccated coconut
60g (1⅓ cup) Rice Bubbles cereal

ICING
450g (3 cups) icing sugar mixture
50g butter, chopped, at room temperature
125ml (½ cup) boiling water
1 tsp vanilla extract

1 Preheat oven to 180°C/160°C fan forced. Line base and sides of a 20 x 30cm slice pan with baking paper.

2 Use electric beaters to beat the butter and caster sugar in a bowl until pale and creamy. Beat in the eggs, 1 at a time, beating well after each addition. Beat in vanilla. Fold in flour and milk until combined. Pour into the prepared pan and smooth surface. Bake for 35-40 minutes or until a skewer inserted into the centre of the cake comes out clean. Cool in pan for 10 minutes then transfer to a wire rack to cool completely.

3 For the white Christmas, place the chocolate in a microwave-safe bowl. Microwave on Medium, stirring every 30 seconds, until melted and smooth. Add the cranberries, coconut and Rice Bubbles. Stir until well combined.

4 Use a large serrated knife to trim the cake edges, then cut the cake in half horizontally. Spread white Christmas mixture over the base cake half, spreading to the edge. Sandwich with the top cake half, cut-side down. Place in the fridge for 15 minutes to firm up slightly. Cut the cake into 15 squares. Place in the fridge for 15 minutes to firm slightly.

5 For the icing, sift the icing sugar into a bowl, then add the butter. Pour the boiling water and vanilla over the butter to melt. Stir until smooth.

6 Spread the shredded coconut over a plate. Use 2 forks to carefully dip a cake square in the icing mixture to coat. Tap on the side of the bowl to remove excess icing. Carefully dip in the coconut, pressing to coat. Transfer to a wire rack. Repeat with the remaining cake squares, icing and coconut. Set aside for 15 minutes or until set. Serve.

COOK'S TIP

These lamingtons are best enjoyed on the day they are made.

○ GLUTEN FREE ○ MAKE AHEAD ○ FREEZABLE ● KID FRIENDLY ○ EASY

★★★★★ *Lamingtons and white Christmas – two of my favourite things… and they work so well together!* **CURLY_SHIRLEY**

STEP-BY-STEP
HOW-TO GUIDE

Learn all our tips and tricks for this fab twist on Aussie lamingtons!

1 Before beginning, make sure the butter is at room temperature to ensure that it becomes aerated. The end result will be a light and fluffy cake.

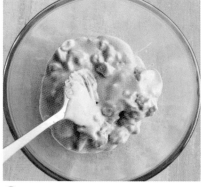

2 When melted in the microwave, chocolate has a tendency to resist dissolving and can burn. To avoid this, stir with a spoon every 30 seconds.

3 Trim the ends first, then halve the cake horizontally. To keep the cake as neat as possible, use a large serrated knife, such as a bread knife.

4 Spread white Christmas over the base cake as close to the edges as possible, then use the back of a spoon to smooth the surface.

5 To make sure the cakes don't get soggy, use 2 forks to hold dunked cake squares over the bowl to allow excess icing to drip off.

6 To make it easier and reduce the mess and waste while coating the cake squares, set up a production line with the coconut near the icing.

★★★★★ *Made these for a fete and they sold out in record time. I'll have to make double next time!* **GARDENINGGAL**

CHOC-CHERRY PROFITEROLE WREATH

Stuff airy pastry puffs with plumes of cream and cherry jam for a show-stopping dessert.

SERVES 12 **PREP** 30 mins (+ cooling & drying) **COOK** 1 hour

100g butter, chopped
330ml (1⅓ cups) water
200g (1⅓ cups) plain flour, sifted
5 eggs, lightly whisked
600ml double cream
600ml thickened cream
1 tsp vanilla extract
200g cherry conserve
680g jar morello sour pitted cherries, drained on paper towel
Chocolate curls, to decorate
Icing sugar, to dust
CHOC-CHERRY SAUCE
200g dark chocolate, finely chopped
60ml (¼ cup) cream
1 tbs brown sugar
2 tbs black cherry bourbon

1 Preheat oven to 190°C/170°C fan forced. Lightly grease 2 baking trays. Draw 20cm circles on 2 sheets of baking paper. Place paper, ink-side down, on prepared trays. Heat the butter and water in a saucepan over medium heat for 1-2 minutes until butter melts and mixture comes to boil. Add flour. Use a wooden spoon to beat for 1-2 minutes or until mixture comes away from the side of the pan. Transfer to a large heatproof bowl. Spread mixture inside bowl to cool slightly.

2 Use electric beaters to beat the eggs into the flour mixture, a little at a time, beating well after each addition, until the mixture is thick and glossy.

3 Spoon half the mixture into a piping bag fitted with a 1.8cm plain round nozzle. Pipe 12 puffs, about 5cm wide, around one of the marked circles, just extending 5mm over the circle, with the rounds touching. Repeat with remaining dough to make a second circle on the remaining tray. Using a finger moistened with water, smooth out any peaks on top of the profiterole puffs.

4 Bake for 45-50 minutes or until puffed and golden. Reduce the heat to 100°C/80°C fan forced. Bake for a further 10 minutes. Turn the oven off. Leave puffs in the oven for at least 1 hour to dry and crisp up. Carefully cut profiterole rings in half horizontally. Discard any pieces of uncooked dough in the centre.

5 Meanwhile, for the choc-cherry sauce, place the chocolate in a heatproof bowl. Heat the cream, sugar and bourbon in a small saucepan over high heat for 3-4 minutes or until sugar dissolves. Pour over the chocolate. Set aside for 5 minutes to melt chocolate. Stir until combined and smooth.

6 Use electric beaters to beat creams and vanilla in a large bowl until firm peaks form. Fold in the conserve to create a swirled pattern. Spoon mixture onto the ring bases. Top with the cherries. Top with remaining pastry halves. Stack profiterole rings on a serving plate. Drizzle with the choc-cherry sauce. Top with chocolate curls and dust with icing sugar to decorate. Serve.

○ GLUTEN FREE ○ MAKE AHEAD ○ FREEZABLE ● KID FRIENDLY ○ EASY

★★★★★ *My Dad loves profiteroles, so this made the perfect centrepiece for his birthday dinner – he loved it!* **ADELE88**

STEP-BY-STEP
HOW-TO GUIDE

Here are the secrets to making a perfect double-decker profiterole wreath.

1 To make sure your profiterole wreaths are perfect circles, use an upturned bowl or plate to draw a guide on the baking paper, then place the paper, marked-side down, on the trays.

2 For perfect puffs, when mixing the choux pastry, add all of the flour at once and cook until the dough leaves the side of the pan to ensure you cook off any excess moisture.

3 When adding the whisked eggs to the choux mixture, add them slowly with the beaters on low speed. If you add them all at once, the mixture will be runny and won't hold its shape.

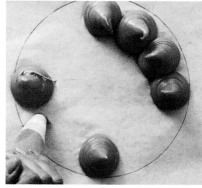

4 For evenly spaced puffs, use the circle like a clock – start piping your puffs at 12 o'clock, then move onto 6, 3 and 9. Then add two puffs between each.

5 Smoothing the peaks that form when you pipe the profiteroles ensures a great finish. Dip your fingertip in warm water to smooth and maintain the glossy dough.

6 After baking, make sure you leave the wreaths in the oven for at least 1 hour to dry and become crisp. Use a large serrated knife to evenly cut them in half horizontally.

★★★★★
Swapped the cherry for strawberry, but otherwise followed the recipe and it was perfect. **MIKEY4359**

CHRISTMAS GINGERBREAD BOMBE ALASKA

Slice into the meringue in this glorious bombe Alaska to reveal layers of spiced gingerbread and rich ice-cream.

SERVES 12 **PREP** 45 mins (+ overnight freezing) **COOK** 25 mins

1L ctn rum and raisin ice-cream, softened slightly
500ml chocolate ice-cream, softened slightly

GINGERBREAD CAKE
300g (2 cups) plain flour
75g (½ cup) self-raising flour
155g (¾ cup, firmly packed) brown sugar
1 tbs ground ginger
1 tsp mixed spice
½ tsp bicarbonate of soda
125g butter, melted
250ml (1 cup) golden syrup
2 eggs, lightly whisked
125ml (½ cup) milk

ITALIAN MERINGUE
315g (1½ cups) caster sugar
125ml (½ cup) water
4 egg whites, at room temperature
Pinch of cream of tartar

1 For the gingerbread cake, preheat oven to 180°C/160°C fan forced. Grease a 24cm x 37.5cm slice pan and line with baking paper. Combine the flours, sugar, ginger, spice and bicarb in a bowl. Stir in the butter, golden syrup, egg and milk. Pour into the prepared pan. Bake for 15 minutes. Cool completely.

2 Cut cake in half crossways. Use the base and top of a 2L pudding basin as a guide to cut out a large disc and small disc of cake. Cut discs in half horizontally. Cut remaining cake in half horizontally, then into 6 triangles.

3 Line pudding basin with 2 layers of plastic wrap, allowing sides to overhang. Place small cake disc in base of basin. Place 3 cake triangles upright up the side of the basin, trimming to fit. Place the remaining cake triangles upside-down in the basin to fit between the upright triangles, trimming to fit. Use any remaining scraps of cake to fill in the gaps between the pieces.

4 Spoon the rum and raisin ice-cream into the cake-lined basin. Use the back of a spoon to make a well in the centre. Place in the freezer for 2 hours or until almost firm.

5 Spoon chocolate ice-cream into the well. Smooth the surface. Cover pudding with the large cake disc, trimming to fit. Cover surface with the overhanging plastic wrap and place in the freezer overnight to set.

6 For the Italian meringue, stir the sugar and water in a saucepan over low heat until the sugar dissolves. Use a wet pastry brush to brush side of pan. Increase heat to medium. Cook for 3-4 minutes until mixture reaches 115°C. Whisk egg whites and cream of tartar in a bowl until soft peaks form. When syrup reaches 120°C, with beaters on low speed, gradually add syrup to eggwhite mixture. Increase speed to high. Whisk for 10 minutes.

7 Carefully lift the bombe from the basin using the overhanging plastic wrap. Turn the pudding onto a serving plate. Roughly spoon the meringue over the cake to cover. Use a cook's blow torch to caramelise. Serve immediately.

○ GLUTEN FREE ● MAKE AHEAD ● FREEZABLE ○ KID FRIENDLY ○ EASY

45 minutes prep

★★★★★

I used vanilla ice-cream instead of the rum and raisin to make it more kid-friendly and everyone loved it!

LEMONLIME19

STEP-BY-STEP
HOW-TO GUIDE

This wow dessert is surprisingly easy, once you know how!

1 Use your pudding basin as a guide to cut out two rounds of cake for the base and top of the bombe, then cut the remaining cake into triangles to line the side of the basin.

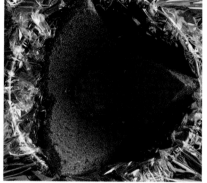

2 It's important to have plastic wrap hanging over the side of the basin for easy removal. Place the small cake round in the base, then line the side with the cake triangles.

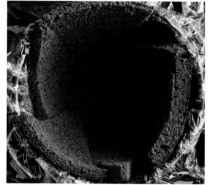

3 Make sure the cake pieces fit well together, as they protect the ice-cream from melting too quickly when torching the meringue. Use scraps to fill any gaps.

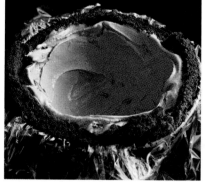

4 It's important that the ice-cream is softened but not melted. Remove the rum and raisin ice-cream from the freezer 10-15 minutes before using, then use to coat the cake with a thick, even layer.

5 If the well in the centre of the ice-cream is melting too fast, place it back in the freezer for 30 minutes to chill. Spoon the chocolate ice cream in, then level the surface before topping with the large cake round.

6 Spoon the meringue over the bomb and use an offset palette knife to create peaks. If you don't have a cook's blow torch, place the bombe on a baking tray. Place in the oven at 200°C/180°C fan forced for 10 minutes.

★ ★ ★ ★ ★

*I cheated and used
store-bought gingerbread
cake and it still worked
out amazing!* **HARMONYPUFFIN**

BÛCHE DE NOËL WITH CARAMEL

Bûche de Noël is all you could wish for in a Christmas cake. With a touch of tradition and a modern feel, it's a light, fun and festive dessert.

SERVES 10 **PREP** 35 mins (+ cooling & setting) **COOK** 30 mins

4 eggs
70g (⅓ cup, firmly packed) brown sugar
100g (⅔ cup) plain flour, sifted
1 tsp ground ginger
½ tsp ground cinnamon
250g ctn mascarpone
125ml (½ cup) thickened cream
2 tbs maple syrup
70g (⅓ cup, firmly packed) brown sugar, extra

TOFFEE NUT BARK
215g (1 cup) caster sugar
125ml (½ cup) water
40g (¼ cup) finely chopped walnuts

1 Preheat oven to 200°C. Grease a 24.5cm x 31cm Swiss roll pan and line with baking paper.

2 Use electric beaters to beat the eggs and sugar in a large bowl until thick and pale, and a ribbon trail forms when the beater is lifted. Fold in the flour, ginger and cinnamon. Spoon mixture into prepared pan and smooth the surface. Bake for 10-12 minutes or until a skewer inserted into the centre comes out clean.

3 Quickly turn cake onto a clean tea towel. Remove paper. Starting at 1 long side, use the tea towel to roll up the hot cake. Transfer to a tray, seam-side down, and allow to cool.

4 Beat mascarpone, cream, maple syrup and extra sugar in a bowl on low speed for 1 minute. Increase speed to medium-high and beat until mixture thickens slightly.

5 Carefully unroll cake. Spread ¾ cup mascarpone mixture evenly over the cake. Roll up. Place, seam-side down, on a plate. Cover with remaining mascarpone mixture. Use the end of a knife to make a tree ring pattern on each end.

6 For the toffee nut bark, stir the sugar and water in a saucepan over low heat until sugar dissolves. Increase heat to high, brushing down side of pan with a wet pastry brush. Bring to the boil. Cook, without stirring, for 8-10 minutes until golden. Remove from the heat. Stir in the walnuts. Pour over a lined baking tray, tilting to thinly spread the toffee. Set aside for 5 minutes to set. Break into shards and arrange slightly overlapping, on the top of the cake.

COOK'S TIP

Both the cake and the toffee can be made up to a day ahead. Store the cake in the fridge and the toffee in an airtight container.

○ GLUTEN FREE ● MAKE AHEAD ○ FREEZABLE ● KID FRIENDLY ○ EASY

STEP-BY-STEP
HOW-TO GUIDE

Prepare this glamorous cake like a pro with our easy steps.

1 Beat the eggs and sugar together until pale and creamy. The mixture should form a 'ribbon trail'. This means that when you lift the whisk, the mixture falls and forms a ribbon that will hold its shape.

2 Line the pan with the edges overhanging slightly – this makes it easier to remove the cake. Use an offset palette knife to ensure the mixture is as smooth as possible. This will make the cake easier to roll.

3 Starting from 1 long side, use the tea towel to help you gently roll up the warm cake and stop it cracking. This initial roll will make it easier to roll the cake after it is filled with the mascarpone mixture.

4 You want to beat the mascarpone mixture until it thickens slightly and has a spreadable consistency. Be careful not to overbeat the mixture, or it may split.

5 Gently unroll the cake and spread evenly with the mascarpone mixture. The cake needs to be completely cooled at this stage, otherwise the filling will melt.

6 Gently roll the cake back up. It's alright if a little of the filling comes out of the cake at this stage, as you will next cover the whole cake with the remaining mascarpone mixture.

★★★★★ *I thought this was going to be tricky, but I found it was fantastic for a culinary-novice like me! It just took a bit of time and it turned out perfectly.* **CHANNYB**

GINGERBREAD HOUSE CAKE

We've taken the hard work out of making a gingerbread house by tucking a cake behind the decorated biscuits to hold them up.

SERVES 12 **PREP** 45 mins (+ chilling & setting) **COOK** 1 hour 10 mins

2 x 540g pkts vanilla cake mix, with frosting sachets

3 tsp ground cinnamon

Desiccated coconut, to decorate

Icing sugar, to dust

GINGERBREAD

100g (½ cup, firmly packed) brown sugar

50g butter

125ml (½ cup) golden syrup

340g (2¼ cups) plain flour, sifted

75g (½ cup) self-raising flour, sifted

1½ tbs ground ginger

1½ tsp mixed spice

½ tsp bicarbonate of soda

1 egg, lightly whisked

330g pkt royal Icing

White pearl beads, to decorate

Silver cachous, to decorate

Sugar stars, to decorate

Candy cane pieces, to decorate

VANILLA FROSTING

200g unsalted butter, at room temperature

345g (2¼ cups) icing sugar mixture

1-2 tbs milk

1 Preheat oven to 170°C/150°C fan forced. Line two 22cm cake pans with baking paper. Make cakes following packet directions, dividing cinnamon between dry ingredients. Bake for 50 minutes. Transfer to a wire rack to cool.

2 To make the gingerbread, place the sugar, butter and golden syrup in a small saucepan over low heat. Cook, stirring constantly, until the butter melts and the sugar dissolves. Set aside for 10 minutes to cool slightly.

3 Combine flours, ginger, mixed spice and bicarb in a large bowl. Add butter mixture and egg. Stir until combined. Turn dough onto a floured surface. Knead until smooth. Divide into 2 portions. Shape into discs. Cover. Place in the fridge for 1 hour.

4 Meanwhile, to make the vanilla frosting, use electric beaters to beat the butter and icing sugar in a bowl until pale and creamy. Add the milk and the frosting sachets from the cake mix, and beat until well combined. Set aside.

5 Trim tops of cakes so they're 4cm high. Place 1 cake, trimmed side down, on a flat plate. Spread ½ cup frosting over the top. Top with remaining cake. Cover top and side with half the remaining frosting. Place the cake in the fridge.

6 To make the gingerbread house template, cut card to 15 x 10cm in size. Draw a rectangle 10cm wide x 8cm high. Along top of rectangle, draw a triangle for the rooftop, making it 5cm high from base of triangle. Cut into house shape.

7 Line 2 baking trays with baking paper. Place a piece of lightly floured baking paper on benchtop. Place 1 dough portion in centre. Place baking paper on top. Roll dough out until 4-5mm thick. Cut out 7 houses using template. Transfer to a prepared tray.

8 Use 3cm shaped cutters to cut out different designs on the houses. Use a small sharp knife to cut out the door shapes. Place the door pieces and shapes on the prepared tray with the houses. Place tray in the fridge for 15 minutes to chill.

9 Preheat oven to 180°C/160°C fan forced. Roll out remaining dough portion and any scraps. Use 10cm and 7.5cm tree cutters to cut out trees. Place on the remaining prepared tray. Bake all pieces for 12 minutes or until golden. Cool for 5 minutes. Transfer to a wire rack.

○ GLUTEN FREE ○ MAKE AHEAD ○ FREEZABLE ● KID FRIENDLY ○ EASY

Prepare the royal icing following the packet directions. Place in a piping bag with a 3mm nozzle. Decorate the front of the houses and trees with icing, white beads, stars, cachous and candy cane pieces. Set aside for 15 minutes to set.

Spread cake with remaining frosting, smoothing the side but making the top rough, to resemble snow. Pipe some royal icing near the base of the cake to help hold houses in place. Stick them along the outside of the cake, joining the edges together.

Pipe the tops on the houses to represent snow on the rooftops. Sprinkle the top of the cake with coconut. Push the trees into the top of the cake. Dust the cake, houses and trees with icing sugar to give it a snowy look.

STEP-BY-STEP
HOW-TO GUIDE

Create a picture-perfect winter gingerbread village around your cake.

1 Use the templates to cut house shapes from the dough and cut closely together to avoid too much re-rolling of dough.

2 Use a small sharp knife and small cookie cutters to cut door shapes and decorative windows from the gingerbread dough.

3 Use the second piece of dough plus any scraps to cut out tree shapes that will create the Christmas forest on top of the cake.

4 Use store-bought royal icing to easily decorate your baked gingerbread pieces and let dry before arranging them around the cake.

5 Reserve some of the frosting to use while decorating the cake with the gingerbread, to make it easy to adhere and stay in place.

6 After arranging the gingerbread houses around the cake, use the remaining royal icing to decorate the roofs of the houses to look like snow.

★★★★★ *This is the ideal dessert to serve a crowd where some people don't care for gingerbread and just want a slice of cake! It was easy to put together and very pretty.* **DANI.BROUGHAM**

CHOC-CHERRY BROWNIE
TRIFLE

This puts the cherry and chocolate flavours of a black forest cake into a trifle, adding fudgy brownie layers to make it extra special.

SERVES 20 **PREP** 1 hour (+ cooling, setting & 4 hours chilling) **COOK** 1 hour 30 mins

1½ x 670g jars sour morello cherries, well drained on paper towel

370g jar cherry conserve

300g dark cooking chocolate, finely chopped

70g unsalted butter

1L thickened cream

2 tbs Frangelico (optional)

2 x 250g ctns mascarpone

1 tsp vanilla bean paste

60g (⅓ cup) icing sugar mixture

150g dark choc melts

200ml dollop cream, lightly whipped

BROWNIES

600g dark cooking chocolate, finely chopped

500g unsalted butter, chopped

6 eggs

4 egg yolks

745g (3½ cups) caster sugar

300g (2 cups) plain flour

95g (1 cup) cocoa powder

1 For the brownies, preheat oven to 160°C/140°C fan forced. Grease two round 20cm (base measurement) cake pans with butter. Line bases with baking paper. Place 300g chocolate and 250g butter in a large microwave-safe bowl. Microwave on High, stirring every minute, until melted. Set aside for 5 minutes to cool slightly.

2 Whisk 3 eggs and 2 egg yolks into the chocolate mixture until combined. Add 370g (1¾ cups) sugar, 150g (1 cup) flour and 50g (½ cup) cocoa. Whisk to combine. Divide between pans. Bake for 35-40 minutes or until a skewer inserted in brownies comes out clean. Set aside for 20 minutes to cool slightly. Transfer to a wire rack to cool completely. Repeat with remaining chocolate, butter, eggs, yolks, sugar, flour and cocoa to make 2 more brownies.

3 Combine cherries and cherry conserve in a bowl and set aside. Place chocolate, butter and 180ml (¾ cup) thickened cream in a small microwave-safe bowl and microwave on Medium, stirring every minute, until melted and smooth. Stir in the Frangelico, if using. Set aside to cool slightly.

4 Use electric beaters to beat mascarpone, vanilla, icing sugar and remaining thickened cream in a bowl. Divide into 3 even portions.

5 Turn an 18cm diameter, 20cm high, 4.25L straight-sided glass bowl upside down over a brownie. Press to make an indent. Use a small sharp knife to cut around indent to trim brownie to fit. Repeat with remaining brownies. Clean bowl.

6 Press one brownie layer into base of bowl. Place chocolate ganache in a snap-lock bag. Snip the end. Drizzle some ganache over brownie, leaving parts exposed. Place one portion of cream mixture in a large piping bag fitted with a 1-2cm plain nozzle. Pipe half the cream over ganache to cover. Spoon over one-third of cherry mixture. Top with remaining cream mixture from piping bag.

7 Cut two of the remaining brownies in half to make semicircles (this makes it easier to place them in the bowl). Place two brownie halves on cream layer. Repeat layering with chocolate ganache, cream, cherry mixture and brownie

○ GLUTEN FREE ● MAKE AHEAD ○ FREEZABLE ● KID FRIENDLY ● EASY

60 minutes prep

halves. Finish with the whole brownie. Top with the remaining ganache. Place in the fridge for 4 hours to set.

8 Meanwhile, line a baking tray with baking paper. Place choc melts in a microwave-safe bowl. Microwave on Medium, stirring every minute, until melted. Set aside for 5 minutes to cool slightly. Spoon into a piping bag and pipe small trees onto the paper, with thick stumps to ensure they stand up once set. Set aside to set. (Place in fridge if it's a hot day.)

9 Remove the trifle from the fridge about 10 minutes before serving. Top with dollop cream and decorate with chocolate trees.

STEP-BY-STEP
HOW-TO GUIDE

Creating our multi-layered trifle is easy with these hints and tips.

1 If your cherries aren't drained well, they can make the trifle too wet. Drain the liquid from the jar, then place cherries on layers of paper towel to remove excess liquid.

2 To trim each brownie to the right size, turn your bowl upside down and press into the top to make an indent. Carefully trim the brownies using the indents to guide you.

3 To keep your trifle layers well defined, clean the sides with damp paper towel after placing each layer in the bowl. The brownies, cherries and cream can all leave streaks on the glass.

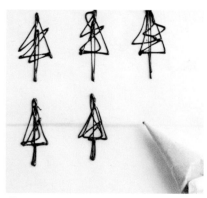

4 Drizzle some chocolate ganache around the edge and surface of each brownie layer. Leave some brownie exposed so that it can soak up the cherry mixture and soften.

5 Chocolate melts hold their shape when they're melted in the microwave. Give them a stir at regular intervals so you can judge how melted they really are.

6 To make a piping bag out of greaseproof paper, roll a square of paper into a cone. Tape the side. Fill with melted chocolate. Snip the end. Use to pipe trees onto baking paper.

FESTIVE & FUN

216

★★★★★

The perfect trifle for Christmas in July. I made it a day ahead and it was superb.

PIEMAKERPARTY

AUSSIE SUMMER GINGERBREAD

We've given a traditional Christmas gingerbread an Aussie summer makeover with this oh-so-cute and easy recipe.

MAKES about 28 **PREP** 45 mins (+ chilling & setting) **COOK** 30 mins

50g butter, chopped
100g (½ cup) brown sugar
125ml (½ cup) honey
1 egg, lightly whisked
300g (2 cups) plain flour
75g (½ cup) self-raising flour
2 tsp ground cinnamon
2 tsp ground ginger
1 tsp ground cloves
½ tsp bicarbonate of soda
2 x 330g pkts royal icing
Food colourings of your choice, to
    tint icing

1 Melt butter with sugar and honey in a small saucepan over low heat. Cool. Combine butter mixture and egg in a bowl. Stir in flours, cinnamon, ginger, cloves and bicarb.

2 Turn dough onto a lightly floured surface and knead until smooth. Divide into 2 discs and cover with plastic wrap. Place in the fridge for 1 hour to rest. Use a lightly floured rolling pin to roll out 1 portion of the dough on a large sheet of baking paper until 4-5mm thick.

3 Preheat oven to 180°C/160°C fan forced. Line 2 baking trays with baking paper. Use a 7cm gingerbread man cutter and a 5.5cm round cutter to cut out shapes. Place on prepared trays. Repeat with remaining dough and leftover dough scraps. Place in the fridge for 15 minutes to chill.

4 Bake for 10-12 minutes until light golden. Cool on trays for 5 minutes then transfer to a wire rack to cool completely.

5 Make royal icing following the packet directions. Divide into bowls. Tint each bowl a different colour of your choice, leaving one bowl white.

6 Place icing in piping bags fitted with 2mm round nozzles. Pipe white outlines on discs and outlines and faces on the gingerbread people. Decorate gingerbread with coloured icing. Allow 15 minutes to completely set.

COOK'S TIP

The finished gingerbread will keep in an airtight container for up to 1 week.

★★★★★ *Absolutely delicious biscuits! They turned out perfect. I did have to grind fresh cloves as I only had whole ones, but that only added to the spicy flavour once baked.* **CHOCOLATEE**

○ GLUTEN FREE ● MAKE AHEAD ○ FREEZABLE ● KID FRIENDLY ● EASY

STEP-BY-STEP
HOW-TO GUIDE

Here's how to make these super-cute Aussie beach gigerbread people.

1 After melting the butter, sugar and honey, it's important to let it cool completely before adding the remaining ingredients, to ensure the dough has the right consistency.

2 Roll the dough out on baking paper and use a lightly floured rolling pin to avoid it sticking. Top with another sheet of baking paper before rolling out if you think it might be too sticky.

3 After cutting out the dough, re-roll the scraps to cut more shapes. Pop it in the fridge for 10-15 minutes beforehand if you think the dough is getting too soft.

4 Use store-bought royal icing to make decorating the gingerbread super-easy. Tint with as many colours as you like, but leave one bowl white.

5 Use the white icing to pipe white outlines on the discs for the beach balls and outlines and faces on the gingerbread people.

6 Use the coloured icing for clothing, adding details with dots or stripes. Fill in discs to make beach balls. Allow at least 15 minutes for the icing to set.

★★★★★
The recipe is fantastic they tasted amazing, although I had to replace the cloves for 1 extra teaspoon of cinnamon and ginger and they still tasted fine. **MADIVCUTE**

GINGERBREAD CHEESECAKE LOAF

Dazzle the crowd with our all-star white chocolate cheesecake topped with a tower of brandy snaps and caramel drizzle!

SERVES 12 **PREP** 1 hour (+ cooling & 6 hours chilling) **COOK** 30 mins

115g (¾ cup) plain flour
50g (⅓ cup) self-raising flour
100g (½ cup, firmly packed)
   brown sugar
2 tsp ground ginger
½ tsp mixed spice
½ tsp bicarbonate of soda
125ml (½ cup) golden syrup
80ml (⅓ cup) olive oil
80ml (⅓ cup) milk
1 egg
200g dark cooking chocolate,
   chopped
125ml (½ cup) thickened cream
Brandy snap twirls, to decorate
   (see page 224)
Caramel sauce, to serve
Ginger biscuits, to crumble

WHITE CHOCOLATE CHEESECAKE
100g butter, melted, plus extra,
   to grease
250g pkt plain chocolate biscuits
2 tbs hot water
1 tbs gelatine powder
3 x 250g pkt cream cheese, at room
   temperature, chopped
250ml (1 cup) thickened cream
155g (¾ cup) caster sugar
180g pkt white chocolate,
   melted, cooled

1 Preheat oven to 180°C/160°C fan forced. Grease a 20 x 30cm Swiss roll pan with melted butter. Line base with baking paper. Combine flours, sugar, ginger, mixed spice and bicarb in a large bowl. Stir in golden syrup, oil, milk and egg. Pour into prepared pan. Bake for 20 minutes or until a skewer inserted into centre comes out clean. Cool in pan. Turn out cake onto a clean work surface. Use a 6cm star cutter to cut 11 stars from cake.

2 For the cheesecake, grease a 7.5cm-deep, 10 x 25cm loaf pan with extra melted butter. Line base and sides with a double layer of baking paper. Process biscuits in a food processor until finely crushed. Add butter. Process until combined. Press mixture over base of prepared pan. Place in fridge to set.

3 Meanwhile, place hot water in a small microwave-safe bowl. Sprinkle with gelatine. Stir until well combined then microwave for 10 seconds or until gelatine dissolves. Stir. Set aside for 1-2 minutes to cool. Place cream cheese, cream and sugar in a food processor. Process until smooth. Add white chocolate. Process until well combined. With motor running, gradually add gelatine mixture.

4 Pour one-third to one-half of cheesecake mixture into the loaf pan. Stand cake stars upright, against each other. Gently push stars into cheesecake mixture in a line down the centre of the pan. Carefully cover with remaining cheesecake mixture. Tap pan on the bench to remove any air pockets. Place in the fridge for 6 hours to set.

5 Remove the cheesecake from the fridge and set aside in pan for 20 minutes. Meanwhile, for the ganache, place the dark chocolate and cream in a microwave-safe bowl. Microwave on High, stirring every minute, until melted and smooth. Set aside for 10 minutes to thicken slightly.

6 Lift the cheesecake out onto a serving platter. Spread top and sides with ganache. Decorate with brandy snaps. Drizzle over caramel and crumble over ginger biscuits to serve.

○ GLUTEN FREE ● MAKE AHEAD ○ FREEZABLE ● KID FRIENDLY ○ EASY

STEP-BY-STEP
HOW-TO GUIDE

Follow these steps to make perfect brandy snap twirls to top your cake.

1 Preheat oven to 180°C/160°C fan forced. Stir 40g softened butter, 55g (¼ cup) brown sugar and 2 tbs golden syrup in a saucepan over low heat until dissolved. Remove from the heat.

2 Sift in 50g (⅓ cup) plain flour and ½ tsp ground ginger. Stir to combine. Pour in 1 tsp brandy. Stir until smooth. Line a baking tray with baking paper.

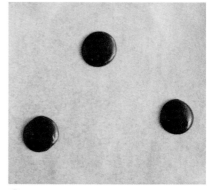

3 Spoon 2 teaspoonfuls of mixture into a disc onto the prepared tray. Repeat 2 more times, leaving room for spreading. Bake for 8 minutes or until bubbling and golden.

4 Rest brandy snaps on the tray for 30 seconds. Use a palette knife to quickly lift and wrap the snaps around a wooden spoon handle, pressing the ends to seal.

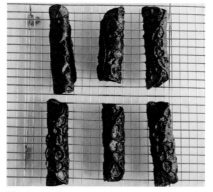

5 Set snaps aside for 1 minute to set then gently slip off the wooden spoon handle and transfer to a wire rack. Repeat with remaining mixture to make 12 snaps.

6 Whisk 125ml (½ cup) thickened cream and 2 tbs double cream in a bowl until firm peaks form. Spoon into a piping bag with a fluted nozzle. Pipe into both ends of the snaps to fill.

★★★★★

What a crazy-good cake!
The stars inside the
cheesecake looked amazing
and the brandy snaps were
a lovely and easy decoration
for something different.

EFFIEBEANS

CHOC MOUSSE STICKY DATE TRIFLE

Topped with golden toffee stars, this fabulously indulgent chocolate twist on Christmas trifle will light up the table.

SERVES 10-12 **PREP** 45 mins (+ cooling & 8 hours chilling) **COOK** 1 hour

250g medjool dates, pitted, finely chopped

1 tsp bicarbonate of soda

100g butter, at room temperature, plus extra melted butter to grease

530g (2½ cups) caster sugar

3 eggs

225g (1½ cups) self-raising flour

¼ tsp ground cinnamon

125ml (½ cup) salted caramel topping, plus extra, to drizzle

60ml (¼ cup) Frangelico (optional)

450ml double cream

185ml (¾ cup) thickened cream

45g (¼ cup) pure icing sugar, sifted, plus extra, to dust

CHOC MOUSSE

360g milk cooking chocolate, finely chopped

375ml (1½ cups) thickened cream

60g butter, chopped

3 eggs, separated

2 tbs pure icing sugar, sifted

400ml double cream

1 Preheat oven to 180°C/160°C fan forced. Grease a 20cm round cake pan and a 20 x 30cm slice pan with melted butter. Line base and sides with baking paper.

2 Place dates and 375ml (1½ cups) water in a saucepan and bring to boil over high heat. Remove from heat. Stir in bicarb. Set aside for 10 minutes to cool.

3 Use electric beaters to beat butter and 215g (1 cup) caster sugar in a bowl until pale and creamy. Add eggs, 1 at a time, beating well after each addition. Add date mixture, flour and cinnamon. Stir until well combined.

4 Divide mixture between prepared pans. Place both pans in oven. Bake the rectangular cake for 20 minutes until a skewer inserted into the centre comes out clean. Bake round cake for 30-35 minutes or until a skewer inserted into centre comes out clean. Transfer to wire racks to cool completely in the pans.

5 Use a large serrated knife to trim round cake to fit in a 3.5L trifle bowl. Place in base of the bowl. Spread top with 80ml (⅓ cup) caramel topping.

6 Use a 7cm star cutter to cut out 8 stars from rectangular cake, reserving offcuts. Place stars around side of trifle bowl. Cut the cake offcuts into 5-8cm pieces and return to the pan. Drizzle with the Frangelico, if using. Set aside.

7 For the mousse, combine the chocolate and thickened cream in a microwave-safe bowl. Microwave, stirring often, for 2-4 minutes until chocolate is melted and mixture is smooth. Add butter and stir until melted. Set aside to cool.

8 Use electric beaters to whisk the egg whites in a clean bowl until soft peaks form. Add icing sugar and whisk until well combined and glossy. Set aside.

9 Use electric beaters with a clean whisk attachment to whisk the egg yolks and double cream into the chocolate mixture until the mixture begins to hold its shape. Gradually fold in the egg white mixture until well combined.

10 Spoon half the mousse into the trifle bowl. Place the soaked cake offcuts on top and press them down until they're almost level with the mousse. Pipe the remaining caramel topping around the inside edge of the bowl.

○ GLUTEN FREE ● MAKE AHEAD ○ FREEZABLE ● KID FRIENDLY ○ EASY

11 Spoon the remaining mousse into the bowl and smooth the surface. Cover with plastic wrap and place in the fridge for 8 hours or overnight to firm.

12 Place the double cream, thickened cream and icing sugar in a bowl. Use a balloon whisk to whisk until soft peaks form. Spoon onto the trifle. Place in the fridge.

13 Place a kitchen broom on your benchtop and weigh down the end so the handle extends out over the floor. Cover the floor with newspaper. Make another batch of toffee following the instructions in Step 13. Remove from the heat. Coat the backs of 2 wooden spoons with toffee. Holding them over the broom handle, press together and quickly pull apart to make strands that fall over the broom handle. Gather the strands, a few at a time while they're still warm and pliable, and twist into a nest. (If the toffee in the pan becomes too hard to use, reheat over low heat to soften slightly.)

14 Arrange the toffee stars (see page 229) on top of the trifle with the toffee nest. Drizzle with extra caramel topping and dust with extra icing sugar.

STEP-BY-STEP HOW-TO GUIDE

Get every element looking (and tasting!) its very best with our tips and tricks.

1 To ensure the cake base fits inside your trifle bowl, place the bowl upside down on top of it and press lightly to make an imprint. Trim the cake following the imprint.

2 The base of a cake is generally flatter, and more sticky, than the top. So, place the cake stars in the bowl with their bases against the glass to make a perfect seal.

3 After adding half the mousse to the bowl, place the soaked cake offcuts in the centre. Press down lightly with the back of a spoon so they're just about level with the mousse.

4 To make a neat line of caramel around the side of the bowl, you're best using a piping bag. Pipe around the edge of the mousse, right up against the glass, for the best effect.

5 Make sure you grease the star cutters well so the toffee is easy to remove. Press the stars out gently, as they can shatter easily. Make a few more than you need, just In case.

6 The toffee needs to be tacky for strands to form. If it's too hot and thin, it'll be hard to use. Holding the spoons together for 30 seconds before pulling them apart helps strands form.

TWIST IT!

To make toffee stars, line a baking tray with baking paper. Spray the inside edges of different-sized star cutters with oil. Place on the tray. Stir 155g (¾ cup) caster sugar and 2 tbs water in a saucepan over low heat, brushing down the side of the pan with a wet pastry brush, until sugar dissolves. Increase heat to high. Bring to the boil. Cook, without stirring, for 5 minutes or until a rich golden colour. Remove from heat and allow bubbles to subside. Carefully spoon toffee into the cutters on the tray. Leave to set. Gently press toffee stars out of the cutters.

EASY TREATS

THESE BEAUTIFUL BITES ARE ALL EASY TO MAKE,
PERFECT FOR A CHEEKY TREAT, IMPROMPTU
MORNING TEA, OR IF YOU JUST WANT TO FILL
THE BISCUIT JAR. GET BAKING!

MILO & BANANA
MUFFINS

MAKES 12 **PREP** 25 mins **COOK** 20 mins

1 Preheat oven to 180°C/160°C fan forced. Line twelve 80ml muffin pans with paper cases.

2 Sift **300g (2 cups) self-raising flour** and **45g (¼ cup) brown sugar** into a bowl. Stir in **95g (⅔ cup) Milo**. Make a well in centre. Whisk **185ml (¾ cup) milk** and **2 eggs** in a jug. Add to flour mixture with **60g cooled melted butter** and **2 mashed bananas**. Fold until just combined.

3 Divide batter among prepared muffin pans. Bake for 20 minutes or until tops spring back when lightly touched. Cool slightly in pans. Transfer to a wire rack. Cool completely.

4 To make the topping, divide **500g chopped cream cheese, at room temperature,** between 2 bowls. Add **2 tbs icing sugar** to 1 bowl and **95g (⅔ cup) Milo** to the other. Using electric beaters, beat each until combined and smooth. Scoop mixtures alternately into a piping bag fitted with a fluted nozzle. Pipe topping onto cooled muffins. Sprinkle with **chocolate curls** or dust with **extra Milo**. Serve.

GOOEY FUNFETTI
BLONDIES

MAKES 20 **PREP** 20 mins **COOK** 45 mins

1 Preheat oven to 180°C/160°C fan-forced. Grease an 18cm x 28cm rectangular slice pan. Line base and sides with baking paper, extending paper 2cm above edges of pan.

2 Stir **100g chopped butter, 180g chopped white chocolate** and **2 tbs milk** in a saucepan over medium heat for 5 minutes or until smooth. Set aside for 10 minutes.

3 Stir in **140g (⅔ cup) caster sugar, 2 lightly beaten eggs, 150g (1 cup) plain flour** and **115g (¾ cup) self-raising flour** until combined. Stir in **⅓ cup sprinkles** until just combined. Spread half the mixture over base of prepared pan. Top with **100g extra white chocolate, cut into 1.5cm pieces,** pushing into mixture. Evenly top with remaining mixture. Scatter with **¼ cup sprinkles**.

4 Bake for 30-35 minutes or until golden and centre is just firm to touch. Cool completely in pan. Cut into squares.

CLASSIC
SCONES

MAKES 16 **PREP** 15 mins **COOK** 20 mins

1 Preheat oven to 220°C/200°C fan forced. Lightly dust a baking tray with flour.

2 Whisk **450g (3 cups) self-raising flour**, **1 tbs caster sugar** (optional) and a **pinch of salt** in a bowl. Rub **60g chilled chopped butter** into flour mixture until fine crumbs form. Make a well in centre and pour in **250ml (1 cup) cold milk**. Use a flat-bladed knife to stir until dough just comes together. Gradually add another **60ml (¼ cup) milk** as necessary, until dough comes together.

3 Turn dough out onto a lightly floured surface. Gently knead for 30 seconds or until just smooth. Press into a 2cm-thick disc. Use a 5cm round cutter to cut out 12 scones. Press leftover dough together. Repeat to make 4 more scones. Place scones, just touching, on prepared tray. Brush with extra milk. Bake for 15-20 minutes or until risen and golden. Transfer to a wire rack to cool. Serve with **strawberry jam**, **whipped cream** and **fairy floss** (optional).

○ GLUTEN FREE ○ MAKE AHEAD ○ FREEZABLE ● KID FRIENDLY ● EASY

PEANUT BUTTER
CUPS

MAKES 24 **PREP** 15 mins **COOK** 25 mins

1 Place **4 choc ripple biscuits** in the microwave and heat on High for 1 minute or until softened. Push softened biscuits into two 12-hole 1½ tablespoon patty pans. Repeat in batches with **20 more choc ripple biscuits**.

2 Preheat oven to 190°C/170°C fan forced. Place **130g (½ cup) smooth peanut butter**, **60ml (¼ cup) sweetened condensed milk**, **1 tbs brown sugar** and **50g butter** in a small saucepan over low heat. Cook, stirring, until melted and smooth. Remove from heat. Set aside to cool. Whisk in **1 egg**. Divide among prepared cases. Bake for 15 minutes or until just set. Cool in pan completely.

3 Place **150g chopped dark chocolate** and **35g butter** in a small heatproof bowl. Microwave for 1 minute or until melted. Stir until smooth. Spoon chocolate mixture over cups. Top each with a **halved square of caramel chocolate**. Set aside to set.

● GLUTEN FREE ● MAKE AHEAD ● FREEZABLE ● KID FRIENDLY ● EASY

LEMON CUSTARD
TEA CAKES

MAKES 30 **PREP** 30 mins (+ cooling) **COOK** 30 mins

1 Place **1½ tbsp custard powder** and **2 tsp caster sugar** in a saucepan. Gradually add **180ml (¾ cup) milk** until smooth. Slowly bring to the boil, stirring. Reduce heat and simmer for 2 minutes. Cool completely, stirring occasionally. Stir through ⅓ cup lemon curd and **grated rind of 1 lemon**.

2 Preheat oven to 180°C/160°C fan forced. Grease a 12 x ½-cup-capacity muffin pan. Use electric beaters to beat **150g chopped butter at room temperature, 100g (½ cup) caster sugar** and **1 tsp vanilla extract** until creamy. Add **2 eggs**, one at a time, beating well. Beat in **200g (1⅓ cups) self-raising flour** and **80ml (⅓ cup) room temperature milk**.

3 Spoon 1 tbs batter into muffin pans, spreading slightly up sides. Add 1 tbs custard then another 1 tbs batter.

4 Bake for 25 minutes or until golden. Cool in pan for 5 minutes. Transfer to a wire rack to cool completely. Serve dusted with **icing sugar**.

○ GLUTEN FREE ● MAKE AHEAD ○ FREEZABLE ● KID FRIENDLY ● EASY

ROCKY ROAD CAKE MIX
COOKIES

MAKES 16 **PREP** 20 mins (+ cooling) **COOK** 10 mins

1 Preheat oven to 180°C/160°C fan forced. Line 2 baking trays with baking paper.

2 Place **440g chocolate cake mix** in a bowl. Add **70g (⅓ cup) dark choc bits, 55g coarsely chopped salted peanuts, 25g (⅓ cup) shredded coconut** and **20g (⅓ cup) mini marshmallows**. Make a well in centre. Add **75g cooled melted butter** and **1 lightly whisked egg**. Stir until combined.

3 Roll heaped tablespoonfuls of mixture into balls. Place on prepared trays, allowing room for spreading. Flatten slightly then bake for 10 minutes. Cool on trays for 5 minutes then transfer to wire racks to cool completely.

4 Place the **icing mix** from the cake packet and **60ml (¼ cup) boiling water** in a bowl. Stir until smooth. Drizzle icing over the biscuits. Working quickly, sprinkle with **extra choc bits, peanuts, coconut** and **marshmallows**. Set aside for 15 minutes or until icing is set. Serve.

○ GLUTEN FREE ● MAKE AHEAD ○ FREEZABLE ● KID FRIENDLY ● EASY

SUPER-EASY
POKE CAKE

SERVES 12 **PREP** 20 mins (+ chilling) **COOK** 45 mins

1 Prepare a **440g butter cake mix** following packet directions and bake in a 20cm square pan in the oven. Set aside to cool. Trim the top.

2 Prepare **85g raspberry jelly crystals** following packet directions. Use a chopstick to poke holes in the top of the cake. Carefully pour in the unset jelly. Cover. Place in the fridge overnight.

3 Top cake with the **prepared icing from the packet** and decorate with **fresh raspberries**.

20 minutes prep

○ GLUTEN FREE ● MAKE AHEAD ○ FREEZABLE ● KID FRIENDLY ● EASY

COCONUT APRICOT
BITES

MAKES 20 **PREP** 20 mins **COOK** 20 mins

1 Preheat oven to 180°C/160°C fan-forced. Line 2 large baking trays with baking paper.

2 Combine **100g finely chopped dried apricots** and **260g (4 cups) shredded coconut** in a large bowl. Add **395g can sweetened condensed milk**. Stir until combined. Using damp hands, shape 2 level tablespoons of mixture into balls. Place balls, 5cm apart, on prepared trays.

3 Bake for 15-18 minutes or until macaroons are lightly browned. Cool completely on trays.

4 Place **100g melted dark chocolate** in a small bowl. Dip the base of 1 macaroon in melted chocolate, allowing excess chocolate to drain off. Return to the tray. Stand for 30 minutes or until set. Serve.

20 minutes prep

● GLUTEN FREE ● MAKE AHEAD ○ FREEZABLE ● KID FRIENDLY ● EASY

15 *minutes prep*

LEMON MERINGUE
POTS

MAKES 4 **PREP** 15 mins **COOK** 10 mins

1 Preheat oven to 200°C/180°C fan forced. Lightly spray four 125ml (½ cup) ovenproof dishes with oil.

2 Place the **finely grated rind of 1 lemon, 100ml fresh lemon juice, 2 tbs honey, 2 tbs gluten-free cornflour** and **2 eggs** in a saucepan and whisk until well combined. Whisk in **100ml water.**

3 Place saucepan over low heat and cook, stirring constantly, for 3-5 minutes until mixture thickens. Remove from heat. Add the **pulp of 2 passionfruit** and stir to combine. Divide mixture among the prepared dishes.

4 Use electric beaters to whisk **2 egg whites** in a clean, dry bowl until soft peaks form. Add **2½ tbs caster sugar,** 1 tbs at a time, whisking constantly until sugar dissolves and mixture is thick and glossy. Spoon mixture over the curd. Bake for 5 minutes or until meringue is golden.

● GLUTEN FREE ○ MAKE AHEAD ○ FREEZABLE ● KID FRIENDLY ● EASY

10 *minutes prep*

PEANUT BUTTER
BROWNIE

SERVES 16 **PREP** 10 mins **COOK** 45 mins

1 Preheat oven to 180°C/160°C fan forced. Grease a 20cm (base measurement) square cake pan and line with baking paper.

2 Place **125g chopped unsalted butter** and **125g chopped dark chocolate** in a heatproof bowl over a saucepan of simmering water (don't let the bowl touch the water). Stir with a metal spoon until melted. Remove from heat. Quickly stir in **3 lightly whisked eggs, 335g (1½ cups) white sugar, 115g (¾ cup) plain flour, 30g (¼ cup) dark cocoa powder, 1 tsp vanilla extract** and a **pinch of salt** until just combined. Pour into prepared pan.

3 Drizzle with **200g (¾ cup) smooth peanut butter.** Use a knife to swirl the peanut butter through the brownie mixture. Bake for 40-45 minutes.

○ GLUTEN FREE ● MAKE AHEAD ○ FREEZABLE ● KID FRIENDLY ● EASY

DOTTY SKILLET
COOKIE

SERVES 8 **PREP** 20 mins (+ cooling) **COOK** 30 mins

1 Preheat oven to 180°C/160°C fan forced. Melt **200g chopped butter** and **200g (1 firmly packed cup) brown sugar** in a 25cm (top measurement) ovenproof enamel or cast iron frying pan over medium-low heat for 1-2 minutes or until combined. Remove from the heat and set aside for 10 minutes to cool slightly.

2 Stir **1 lightly whisked egg** and **2 tsp vanilla essence** into the butter mixture. Sift **225g (1½ cups) plain flour**, **30g (¼ cup) cocoa powder** and **1 tsp bicarbonate of soda** into the pan. Add **35g (⅓ cup) desiccated coconut**. Stir gently to combine. Smooth surface and sprinkle with **mixed coated chocolate buttons**. Bake for 25 minutes or until crisp. Set aside to cool in pan before cutting into wedges.

20 minutes prep

○ GLUTEN FREE ● MAKE AHEAD ○ FREEZABLE ● KID FRIENDLY ● EASY

PEAR
PASTRIES

SERVES 4 **PREP** 15 mins **COOK** 25 mins

1 Preheat oven to 220°C/200°C fan forced. Line 2 baking trays with baking paper. Peel, halve and core **2 Packham pears**. Thinly slice lengthways, leaving stem-end intact.

2 Cut out discs from **1-2 puff pastry sheets** a little larger than the pears. Use a small sharp knife to mark a 1cm-wide border around the inside edge of the pastry, without cutting through. Brush each with **1 tsp marmalade**. Top with pear. Brush edges with **1 lightly whisked egg**. Place on the prepared trays and bake for 20-25 minutes until golden. Serve with **double cream**, **maple syrup** and **chopped toasted hazelnuts**.

15 minutes prep

○ GLUTEN FREE ○ MAKE AHEAD ○ FREEZABLE ○ KID FRIENDLY ● EASY

MINI FAIRY SHORTBREAD

BITES

MAKES 64 **PREP** 30 mins **COOK** 15 mins

1 Preheat oven to 180°C/160°C fan forced and line 2 baking trays with baking paper.

2 Pulse **300g (2 cups) plain flour**, **60g (⅓ cup) icing sugar mixture**, **200g chopped chilled butter** and **1 tsp vanilla extract** in a food processor in short bursts until fine crumbs form.

3 Add **60ml (¼ cup) iced water**. Process until mixture just comes together (you may need to add extra water). Turn dough out onto a floured surface. Gently knead until smooth.

4 Roll out dough between 2 sheets of baking paper to form a 7mm-thick rectangle. Cut dough into 5cm squares. Cover dough with **hundreds and thousands**, using a rolling pin to press gently into the surface.

5 Transfer squares to prepared trays. Cut each in half diagonally. Pull apart slightly. Bake for 15 minutes or until golden underneath and cooked through. Transfer to a wire rack to cool. Serve.

○ GLUTEN FREE ● MAKE AHEAD ○ FREEZABLE ● KID FRIENDLY ● EASY

CHOC-RASPBERRY MAGIC

SLICE

SERVES 10 **PREP** 15 mins **COOK** 55 mins

1 Preheat oven to 160°C/140°C fan forced. Line a 16 x 26cm slice pan with baking paper, allowing the long sides to overhang.

2 Cut **450g store-bought choc chip cookie dough** into 15 slices. Place the slices in even rows in the prepared pan. Use your fingertips to press dough together and cover the base. Bake for 25 minutes or until golden.

3 Spread **160g (½ cup) raspberry jam** on top of the cookie dough. Sprinkle with **225g coconut flakes**. Drizzle **395g can sweetened condensed milk** over the top to coat. Top with **125g fresh raspberries, 95g (½ cup) dark choc bits** and **95g (½ cup) white choc bits**. Bake for 30 minutes or until golden around the edges and set. Drizzle with **melted dark chocolate** (optional).

● GLUTEN FREE ● MAKE AHEAD ● FREEZABLE ● KID FRIENDLY ● EASY

BROWNIE CARAMEL
BITES

MAKES 24 **PREP** 20 mins **COOK** 15 mins

1 Preheat oven to 180°C/160°C fan forced. Line 24 mini muffin pans with paper cases.

2 Place **125g chopped dark chocolate** and **125g chopped unsalted butter** in a heatproof bowl over a saucepan of simmering water (don't let the bowl touch the water). Stir with a metal spoon until melted. Remove from the heat. Quickly stir in **3 lightly whisked eggs, 335g (1½ cups) white sugar, 150g plain flour, 2 tbs cocoa powder** and a **pinch of salt** until just combined. Spoon mixture among the cases. Bake for 15 minutes or until firm to touch. Set aside for 5 minutes, then transfer to a wire rack to cool completely.

3 Top each brownie bite with a spoonful of **dulce de leche or caramel spread** and sprinkle with **dark chocolate curls** to decorate.

20 minutes prep

● MAKE AHEAD ● ● KID FRIENDLY ● EASY

PAVLOVA LAMINGTON
KISSES

MAKES 16 **PREP** 30 mins (+ cooling) **COOK** 40 mins

1 Preheat oven to 90°C/70°C fan forced. Use 4cm round cutter to draw 32 circles, 2cm apart, on 2 sheets of baking paper. Place, pencil-side down, on 2 baking trays.

2 Use electric beaters to beat **2 egg whites, at room temperature**, in a bowl until stiff peaks form. Gradually add **100g (½ cup) caster sugar**, 1 tbs at a time, whisking well after each addition, until mixture is thick and glossy.

3 Spoon meringue into a piping bag fitted with a 1.5cm round nozzle. Pipe to fill circles. Sprinkle with **25g (⅓ cup) shredded coconut**. Bake for 40 minutes or until crisp. Turn oven off. Cool meringues in oven, with door slightly ajar.

4 Line a tray with baking paper. Gently sandwich 2 meringue bases with a small scoop of **slightly softened gluten-free chocolate ice-cream**. Place on prepared tray. Repeat to make 16 kisses. Scatter with **extra coconut**. Drizzle with **melted dark chocolate**. Set aside for 5 minutes to set. Place in the freezer until ready to serve.

30 minutes prep

● GLUTEN FREE ● MAKE AHEAD ○ FREEZABLE ● KID FRIENDLY ● EASY

15 minutes prep

PAV IN A
CUP

MAKES 6 **PREP** 15 mins **COOK** 35 mins

1 Preheat oven to 140°C/120°C fan forced. Lightly grease six 250ml (1 cup) ovenproof cups or ramekins and dust lightly with cornflour.

2 Use electric beaters to beat **4 egg whites** in a clean dry bowl until soft peaks form. Gradually beat in **215g (1 cup) caster sugar**, 1 tbs at a time, until mixture is thick and glossy and sugar has dissolved. Fold in **3 tsp gluten-free cornflour** and **1 tsp white vinegar** until just combined. Spoon mixture among cups. Bake for 30-35 minutes or until crisp. Turn oven off. Leave in oven with door slightly ajar to cool completely.

3 Use a balloon whisk to lightly whisk **300ml double cream** in a bowl until just firm. Lightly crush **125g fresh or frozen raspberries** with a fork and fold through the cream. Top pavlovas with the cream mixture and **white chocolate curls**.

● GLUTEN FREE ○ MAKE AHEAD ○ FREEZABLE ● KID FRIENDLY ● EASY

20 minutes prep

FRYING PAN CHOC-CHIP
COOKIE

SERVES 8 **PREP** 20 mins (+ cooling) **COOK** 45 mins

1 Preheat oven to 170°C/150°C fan-forced. Using an electric mixer, beat **150g softened butter, 2 tsp vanilla extract, 200g (1 firmly packed cup) brown sugar** and **70g (⅓ cup) caster sugar** until smooth. Add **2 eggs**, 1 at a time, beating to combine after each addition. Fold in **225g (1½ cups) plain flour, 75g (½ cup) self-raising flour, 125ml (½ cup) milk, 110g (⅔ cup) roughly chopped salted roasted peanuts** and **100g chopped dark chocolate**.

2 Grease a 5cm-deep, 20.5cm round (base) heavy-based ovenproof frying pan. Spread mixture into the prepared pan. Smooth top. Scatter with **100g chopped dark chocolate**. Bake for 40 to 45 minutes or until firm around the edges. Stand, uncovered, for 20 minutes. Serve warm with **vanilla ice-cream**.

○ GLUTEN FREE ○ MAKE AHEAD ○ FREEZABLE ● KID FRIENDLY ● EASY

ICED LEMON SHORTBREAD
SLICE

SERVES 12 **PREP** 25 mins **COOK** 25 mins

1 Preheat oven to 170°C/150°C fan-forced. Grease an 18 x 28cm slice pan. Line base and sides with baking paper, extending paper 2cm above edges of pan.

2 Using electric beaters, beat **250g softened butter**, **3 tsp finely grated lemon rind** and **1 tsp vanilla extract** until light and fluffy. Gradually beat in **150g (1 cup) icing sugar mixture**. Add **1 egg**. Beat until combined. Beat in **300g (2 cups) plain flour**, in 2 batches. Spoon into prepared pan. Use damp hands to press mixture to cover base evenly.

3 Bake for 20-25 minutes or until edges just start to turn golden and top is just firm. Cool completely in pan.

4 Using electric beaters, beat **150g softened butter** and **2 tsp finely grated lemon rind** until light and fluffy. Gradually beat in **450g (3 cups) icing sugar mixture** until smooth. Beat In **1½ tbs lemon juice**. Spread with icing. Decorate with **lemon rind**. Cut into pieces.

○ GLUTEN FREE ● MAKE AHEAD ○ ... ● KID FRIENDLY ● EASY

25 minutes prep

GINGER
SNAPS

MAKES 34 **PREP** 30 mins (+ chilling) **COOK** 20 mins

1 Line 2 baking trays with baking paper. Combine **375g (2½ cups) self-raising flour**, **1 tsp baking powder**, **3 tsp ground ginger**, **1 tsp ground cinnamon**, **½ tsp ground cardamom** and **¼ tsp ground cloves** in a large bowl.

2 Combine **180g butter**, **1 cup (200g) brown sugar** and **60ml (¼ cup) treacle** in a saucepan over low heat. Cook, stirring, for 3 minutes or until smooth. Set aside for 5 minutes to cool slightly. Add to the flour mixture with **1 lightly whisked egg** and stir until well combined. Cover with plastic wrap and place in the fridge for 2 hours or until firm.

3 Preheat oven to 180°C/160°C fan-forced. Place **110g (½ cup) demerara sugar** on a large plate. Roll tablespoonfuls of dough into balls. Roll in sugar to coat. Place on prepared trays. Press each to flatten to a 4cm disc. Bake, swapping trays halfway, for 12-15 minutes or until golden. Set aside on trays to cool completely.

● ... ● MAKE AHEAD ● ... ● KID FRIENDLY ● EASY

30 minutes prep

GLUTEN-FREE
LEMON BAR

MAKES 16 **PREP** 20 mins (+ cooling) **COOK** 40 mins

1 Preheat oven to 180°C/160°C fan forced. Line a 16 x 26cm (base measurement) slice pan with baking paper, allowing the sides to overhang.

2 Combine **100g (½ cup) caster sugar**, **75g (½ cup) gluten-free plain flour**, **55g (½ cup) almond meal** and **45g (½ cup) desiccated coconut** in a bowl. Stir in **100g melted unsalted butter**. Press firmly and evenly into prepared pan. Bake for 15 minutes or until light golden.

3 To make the filling, whisk **4 eggs**, **35g (¼ cup) gluten-free plain flour** and **215g (1 cup) caster sugar** in a medium bowl until smooth. Whisk in **finely grated rind of 1 lemon** and **125ml (½ cup) fresh lemon juice**.

4 Pour filling over base. Bake for 20-25 minutes or until filling is set. Cool completely in pan before cutting into bars and dusting with **icing sugar**. Decorate with **small lemon slices** and **piped whipped cream**, if using.

● GLUTEN FREE ● MAKE AHEAD ● FREEZABLE ● KID FRIENDLY ● EASY

20 minutes prep

BUTTERY COOKIES WITH
FUNFETTI

MAKES 45 **PREP** 20 mins (+ cooling) **COOK** 20 mins

1 Preheat oven to 180°C/160°C fan-forced. Grease 4 large baking trays and line with baking paper.

2 Sift **225g (1½ cups) plain flour**, **½ tsp cream of tartar** and **½ tsp bicarbonate of soda** into a large bowl. Stir in **55g (¾ cup) caster sugar**. Add **115g cooled melted butter**, **1 tsp vanilla extract** and **1 lightly beaten egg**. Mix well. Stir in **30g (¼ cup) sprinkles**. Roll 2 level teaspoonfuls of mixture into balls. Place on prepared trays, 5cm apart. Flatten slightly. Top liberally with **extra sprinkles**.

3 Bake biscuits, 2 trays at a time, for 10 minutes, swapping position of trays halfway through cooking, or until just firm to touch but not browned. Cool on trays for 5 minutes. Transfer to a baking paper-lined wire rack to cool.

● GLUTEN FREE ● MAKE AHEAD ● FREEZABLE ● KID FRIENDLY ● EASY

20 minutes prep

TRADITIONAL
ANZACS

MAKES 26 **PREP** 25 mins **COOK** 15 mins

1 Preheat oven to 180°C/160°C fan forced. Line 2 baking trays with baking paper.

2 Combine **150g (1 cup) plain flour**, **155g (¾ cup) caster sugar**, **140g (1½ cups) rolled oats** and **80g (1 cup) moist coconut flakes** in a bowl. Make a well in the centre. Add **120g melted butter** and **60ml (¼ cup) golden syrup**. Combine **½ tsp bicarbonate of soda** and **1 tbs boiling water** in a bowl. Add to well. Stir until combined.

3 Roll tablespoonfuls of mixture into balls. Place, 5cm apart, on the prepared trays. Flatten slightly. Bake for 12-15 minutes or until golden brown. Cool on trays.

25 minutes prep

○ GLUTEN FREE ● MAKE AHEAD ● FREEZABLE ● KID FRIENDLY ● EASY

BERRY CHEESECAKE
TACOS

SERVES 12 **PREP** 20 mins **COOK** 20 mins

1 Preheat oven to 180°C/160°C fan forced. Place **4 flour tortillas** on a work surface. Use a round 8cm-diameter pastry cutter to cut 3-4 discs from each tortilla.

2 Sift **70g (⅓ cup) caster sugar** and **½ tsp ground cinnamon** onto a plate. Brush both sides of 6 tortilla discs with **20g melted butter**. Dip into the sugar mixture. Turn to coat. Place upright between holes of an upturned muffin pan. Bake for 8 minutes or until golden. Set aside for 3 minutes to cool slightly before transferring to a wire rack to cool completely. Repeat with **20g melted butter**, remaining tortilla discs and sugar mixture to make 12 taco shells.

3 Spoon **230g tub Philadelphia Classic Icing** into a sealable plastic bag. Snip off 1 corner, 1cm from end. Pipe icing into each taco shell. Top with **250g chopped fresh strawberries**. Sprinkle with **toasted shredded coconut**.

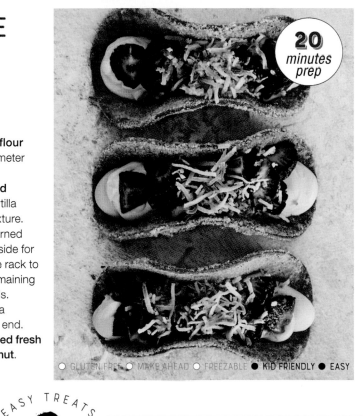

20 minutes prep

○ GLUTEN FREE ○ MAKE AHEAD ○ FREEZABLE ● KID FRIENDLY ● EASY

○ GLUTEN FREE ● MAKE AHEAD ○ FREEZABLE ● KID FRIENDLY ● EASY

CARAMEL & RASPBERRY
PALMIERS

MAKES 48 **PREP** 30 mins **COOK** 20 mins

1 Preheat oven to 210°C/190°C fan forced and line 2 baking trays with baking paper.

2 Place **2 just-thawed sheets frozen puff pastry** on a work surface. Spread 1 sheet with **1 heaped tbs raspberry jam**. Combine **1 heaped tbs caramel spread** and **a pinch of salt** in a bowl. Spread over remaining pastry sheet. Sprinkle each sheet with **15g desiccated coconut**.

3 Working with 1 pastry sheet at a time, fold 2 opposite sides into centre. Repeat folding in sides. Fold in half lengthways to form a log. Cut crossways into 1cm-thick slices. Place, cut-side up, on prepared trays, allowing room for spreading. Bake for 15-20 minutes or until golden. Cool on trays.

4 Spread **melted white chocolate** over half the raspberry palmiers. Dip remainder halfway in white chocolate. Spread **melted dark chocolate** over half the caramel palmiers. Dip remainder halfway in dark chocolate. Chill for 10 minutes to set.

2-INGREDIENT ICE-CREAM
MUFFINS

MAKES 12 **PREP** 5 mins (+ cooling) **COOK** 15 mins

1 Preheat oven to 180°C/160°C fan forced. Line twelve 80ml (⅓ cup) muffin pans with paper cases.

2 Place **750ml (3 cups) slightly softened strawberries and cream ice-cream**, and **225g (1½ cups) self-raising flour** in a large bowl. Stir until well combined. Spoon the mixture evenly into the prepared muffin pans. Bake for 12-15 minutes or until a skewer inserted in the centres comes out clean. Transfer to a wire rack to cool completely.

3 Top each muffin with a **scoop of ice-cream**, **chopped fresh strawberries** and **chocolate sprinkles** (optional).

○ GLUTEN FREE ○ MAKE AHEAD ○ FREEZABLE ● KID FRIENDLY ● EASY

ICE-CREAM CONE
PINATAS

MAKES 8 **PREP** 25 mins **COOK** 1 hour

1 Preheat oven to 140°C/120°C fan forced. Trace around tops of **8 mini waffle cones** on a sheet of baking paper, allowing 5cm between each. Place, ink-side down, on a baking tray.

2 Use electric beaters to whisk **2 egg whites** until soft peaks form. Gradually add **100g (½ cup) caster sugar**, 1 tbs at a time, beating constantly until sugar dissolves and mixture is thick. Spoon **60g cooled melted dark chocolate** over meringue (do not stir). Transfer to a piping bag fitted with a 1cm fluted nozzle. Pipe into circles. Bake for 30 minutes. Reduce oven to 120°C/100°C fan forced. Bake for 30 minutes or until crisp. Transfer to a wire rack to cool completely.

3 Stand cones upright in a narrow glasses. Fill with **assorted lollies**. Working 1 at a time, spread **melted dark choc melts** over base and slightly up side of a meringue. Place on a cone, choc-side down. Hold until just set. Spread more **melted choc** around edge of meringue and cone. Sprinkle with **chocolate sprinkles**. Return to glass until set.

○ GLUTEN FREE ○ MAKE AHEAD ○ FREEZABLE ● KID FRIENDLY ● EASY

MADELEINES WITH CHOC
DRIZZLE

MAKES 12 **PREP** 15 mins **COOK** 10 mins

1 Preheat oven to 180°C/160°C fan forced. Grease twelve 40ml madeleine pans with melted butter. Dust with plain flour and shake out excess.

2 Use electric beaters to beat **70g (⅓ cup) caster sugar**, **1 tsp finely grated orange rind** and **1 egg** in a bowl for 2 minutes or until pale and creamy. Sift in **75g (½ cup) plain flour** and **½ tsp baking powder**. Drizzle **90g cooled melted butter** down edge of bowl into orange mixture. Fold until just combined. Transfer half the batter to a separate bowl.

3 Sift **1 tbs dark cocoa powder** into 1 bowl of batter. Stir until just combined. Spoon into 1 end of the madeleine pans. Rest edge of pan on a chopping board to allow mixture to sit on an angle. Spoon plain mixture over the top.

4 Bake for 8-10 minutes or until madeleines spring back when lightly pressed in the centre. Cool in pan slightly. Transfer to a wire rack to cool completely. Dust with **icing sugar** and drizzle over **melted dark chocolate**. Serve.

○ GLUTEN FREE ○ MAKE AHEAD ○ FREEZABLE ● KID FRIENDLY ● EASY

INDEX

USE OUR HANDY INDEX FOR EVERYTHING YOU NEED
TO KNOW FROM KEY GUIDES TO MAIN INGREDIENTS.

Baking Masterclass

ALPHABETICAL INDEX

Looking for a favourite recipe? Here's a list of every recipe in this book to make it easier to find the ones you want to cook again and again.

Baking Masterclass

Whether you want a freezable, make-ahead dessert, a kid-friendly cake, an easy bake or a gluten-free treat, look no further.

● MAKE AHEAD

Baking Masterclass

Maybe you're making something for the chocoholic in your life, have a craving for caramel or want to use up those spices? The right recipe is right here.

editor-in-chief Brodee Myers
executive editor, mass food Daniela Bertollo
food director Michelle Southan
book food editor Tracy Rutherford
magazine food editors Alison Adams, Elisa Pietrantonio,
Katrina Woodman
creative director Giota Letsios
art director Natasha Barisa
book art director Sarah Cooper
book subeditor Francesca Percy
design concept Rachelle Napper, Brush Media
editorial coordinator Bonnie Moorhouse

managing director – food and travel Fiona Nilsson

HarperCollins*Publishers* Australia
publishing director Brigitta Doyle
head of Australian non-fiction Helen Littleton
managing editor adult books Belinda Yuille

CONTRIBUTORS

Recipes

Alison Adams, Sonja Bernyk, Kerrie Carr, Kim Coverdale,
Chrissy Freer, Marion Grasby, Sarah Hobbs, Kathy Knudsen,
Cathie Lonnie, Liz Macri, Tiffany Page, Louise Patniotis,
Miranda Payne, Elisa Pietrantonio, Kerrie Ray,
Tracy Rutherford, Justine Schofield, Michelle Southan,
Katrina Woodman

Photography

Guy Bailey, Steve Brown, Ben Dearnley, Chris Jones,
Vanessa Levis, Nigel Lough, Cath Muscat, Al Richardson,
Jeremy Simons, Brett Stevens, Craig Wall, Andrew Young

HarperCollins*Publishers*
Australia • Brazil • Canada • France • Germany • Holland
• Hungary • India • Italy • Japan • Mexico • New Zealand
• Poland • Spain • Sweden • Switzerland • United Kingdom
• United States of America

First published in Australia in 2021
by HarperCollins*Publishers* Australia Pty Limited
ABN 36 009 913 517
harpercollins.com.au

A catalogue record for this book is available from the
National Library of Australia.

ISBN 978 1 4607 5993 6

Colour reproduction by Splitting Image Colour Studio,
Clayton, Victoria, Australia

Printed and bound in China by RR Donnelley

8 7 6 5 4 3 2   22 23 24

THANK YOU

At taste.com.au HQ, we love creating crowd-pleasing bakes! The *Baking.Masterclass* cookbook is full of amazing recipes and all the tips and know-how you need to create the most stunning cakes, biscuits, puddings and more. We'd like to thank everyone on the Taste team who contributed to this book – from our foodies to photographers, stylists, designers, subeditors and the digital team. Each recipe is a result of their amazing passion and teamwork.

A huge thank you as well to Brigitta Doyle and Helen Littleton, our partners at HarperCollins. We're very thankful for your expertise and support.

We'd also like to thank... you, the audience of taste.com.au! Thousands of passionate cooks visit our site every day to plan, cook and share their reviews, ratings and recipe twists and tips. We love hearing about your passion for cooking and the gusto with which you make our recipes, so keep those reviews, comments and photos coming.